LIVING OFF THE HUSTLE

LIVING OFF THE HUSTLE

ANUNG VILAY

Courageous Creativity

Copyright © 2021 Anung Vilay
Courageous Creativity™

All rights reserved. No part of this book may be reproduced or used in any manner without the prior written permission of the copyright owner, except for the use of brief quotation in a book review

To request permission, contact anung@courageouscreativity.co

Paperback:978-1-7363008-0-0
Ebook:978-1-7363008-1-7

The information in this book was correct at the time of publication, but the Author does not assume any liability for loss or damage caused by errors or omissions.

Printed by Ingram Sparks

To my parent
For letting me explore and not making me
feel like a failure with all my
experimenting. Just asking "what are you
doing now?"

CONTENTS

Dedication   v

Intro	1
Why Start A Side Hustle	8
Mindset	17
Going On Your Own Or Getting Help	36
Finding Ideas	42
Active Vs Passive	56
Marketing	63
How To Price Your Work & Make A Profit	76
Taxes And Protecting Yourself	83
Legal	94
Multiple Streams Of Income	104
Setting Up Systems	113
How To Hire Help	126

Conclusion 135

Appendix I 137
Appendix II 139
Bio 141

Intro

Not going to lie, I've read a lot of self-help and business books. And I've gotten a lot of great info from most of them. But man, I'm tired of hearing the same things over and over, especially, where most of them have years of working experience in a high paying corporate job before quitting to start their businesses.

What about those of us who never wanted to go into corporate? Who got stuck in jobs that rarely gave us full-time hours? Who were looking for something else that we couldn't quite grasp?

We don't want any more corporate thinking. Even those who have successful side hustles and businesses still tout that same "wisdom" from their old jobs.

Sadly, most of us can't make a business successful right out of high school or college. So, we need to take up some work just to survive. However, we want to make something that's ours so that we can keep our freedom.

Because this new 'Hustle' Economy is different. You can make more money from a Side Hustle than from a crappy customer service job. You can actually have several Side Hustles that you can live off of. Or not even worry about being bored with season Hustles.

I've done it all. Everything in the pursuit of never settling and a general dislike at being told I can't do something. I have been working in Customer Service since I was 15 years of age. I did a lot of exploring in what 'job' would be perfect for me.

At the end of college, I realized that most of the paths before me were restricting. I didn't want to go into more debt to get one of those "guaranteed" high paying jobs. (Yes, I'm rolling my eyes too.) After college, I took the time to explore different alternatives.

Even in that area, there were prescribed avenues. Blogger, writer, speaker, and graphic designer were some of the options. Those were so specific, especially for women. Not gonna lie, I did try the blogger route. Sure as hell couldn't be a mom blogger. Since I was missing a key ingredient there, children.

I never could have a "normal" job. I went back and forth between entry-level ones trying to figure out what direction to take. I even applied for grad school in the hopes of teaching at the academic level.

All because I was told that I needed 1 full-time job to live on. That college would set me up for life. That it would be easy to find job security.

What a load of crap!

I graduated a couple of years after the 2008 bust and there were still people out there telling everyone that nothing is wrong. That nothing has changed. The old rules still applied.

I'm so glad I didn't listen.

The summer after I graduated, I took a cafe job in a hotel which was perfect for my weird-ass. I had no problem waking up at 3:30 in the morning to work by myself making specialty coffee drinks for power-hungry business people. They were actually nice, tipped great, and I got off at 10 am.

Great to have all that free time...but everyone else either had 'careers' or crap jobs with crap hours. So, no one was available when I was free. So, I had plenty of time to read. By choice. I love to read.

And in that time, I explored so many different sections. The idea of writing for a living never crossed my mind until then. This is until I finally gathered the courage to look at all the Writer's Digest books which really opened my mind. (Yeah, it took me years to finally get something out, but that's another story).

But the book that really changed my outlook and trajectory was Barbara Winter's, Making a Living Without a Job. It opened my eyes to not having to have a "job". To not have to work full-time at one thing. That I could have dozens and when I got tired of one I could just discard it.

It was unheard of at that time. We were always told to get the one job and stick with it. Luckily, things were changing. As my generation was getting out into the world we didn't stick around at bad jobs.

We weren't going to sell our souls to the corporate overlords.

And through the years I did a lot of trial and error on finding what was my sweet spot on all my revenue streams. Here are some of the things I've tried:

- Work at a bookstore (multiple time), cafe, hotel,

snow tube attendant, video editor, and a crappy big box store that are horrible to its employees
- Dog walking, babysitting, PCA, copywriter, social media manager, photographer, fun race set-up, ticket taker
- Content creator, podcaster, writer, event coordinator, apparel designer, consultant, shop manager

These are broken down into part-time employment, contract or freelance work, and your own work and creation. The best way to make a full-time income from all your side hustles is to have a mixture of all three.

I average having four hustles in a week. Sometimes doing freelance computer work in the morning then heading out to the bookstore for a closing shift. Even with running my business now I still have that many hustles going too. They just only take 1-3 days to work on, and never more than a few hours each day.

We have all been taught that there is supposed to be "one thing" out there that we are meant to do. That passion, that spark, the one thing that will give meaning to our life.

And it's a load of more crap!

Really sucks, huh?

That all those years of searching were for nothing. Those years of schooling, or training, or just trying everything. With many times thinking you might have found it.

But when those weren't perfect, you pushed them aside. No matter if you enjoyed them or not. Or if you actually got some good skills from it. It was not "the one" so it must be put aside.

Well, I didn't want to do that. And neither do you.

Some people will never have something that they will have an undying passion for. I know, shocker. And that isn't a bad thing. Though so many business books out there are really good, they are built on the assumption that what you build will be all-consuming. Yeah, you want your doctor to be an expert with many years of experience. I want those bridges to not be 'meh, good enough'.

And I'm not built that way.

A lot of you out there are not either. There is nothing wrong with building something that makes you an extra few thousand over the summer. Something over the holiday season so you can take your family on a great vacation every year. The idea that any business you build is a failure if you're not making multiple six figures.

Now let me preface that whatever side hustle you do (or more, I vote for more) you should actually enjoy it. There's enough in life to make us miserable, we don't need to purposefully add it ourselves. Mostly, enjoying the time you're making money should not be mutually exclusive things.

Don't listen to the crap out there that you should be wildly passionate about whatever you create. And that it should be making you hundreds of thousands a year. While I love hearing stories of people beating the odds and being hugely successful, it's not for everyone.

Always looking for something that's passion can actually block you to all the possibilities. Getting started you may be okay with not being miserable. This does not need to be your end-all-be-all doing this the rest of your life purpose.

Now, I like reading Gary Vaynerchuk's books and listening to his podcast, but I can't use everything he gives. Mostly because I don't have the drive to make something so big (though I do recommend some of his work. He has some great info that anyone can use.)*

My passion wasn't something that came to me suddenly. It was not this fully formed piece of me that I needed to find. It took all my life to get to where I am. And it will keep coming with more time.

Yes, I've wanted to write a book for years. Actually, make a living from it. But I wasn't a good writer from the beginning. (I'm not sure I'm much good right now. Maybe decent at editing.)

But this stemmed from my love of books and that wasn't something I loved all my life. Hell, I was actually several levels behind in reading skills until junior high.

Before that, it came from my enjoyment of stories. Not in the high-brow way of the sophisticated story. But wanting to hear the stories of my family from their home country. Or just the adventures of my friends from over the weekend. Fantastical adventures and sweet romances.

All of those built on each other and have helped and influenced a lot of the work I've done. Not just in writing this. In the different blog posts and outlining podcast episodes and especially working part-time at Barnes and Noble.

And a lot of people who try to help others in this realm help others who already have a good-paying career. People who want to "replace" 6 figure incomes. People have been successful in their chosen careers for years.

None of that fit me. I was a Jack of all trades. Taking work wherever I could, to try and pay the bills. Mostly because I was still trying to figure out what I wanted to do with my life. Going to Grad school wasn't an option. I sure as hell didn't want to go into teaching. That old wisdom that a college degree would guarantee you a good-paying job was bullshit by then.

So, I spent a lot of time wandering. Moved around, different jobs, experimenting with different things. All I knew is that I didn't want to be stuck hating every moment I was working. I was not going to fall into the group that believed it was perfectly fine to be miserable at your job. But it did give idea on what I didn't want to do.

That it's normal to never want to get out of bed in the morning. Needing a gallon of coffee just to get going. Missing out on important times in your life and family for work. Or even just not enjoying life until you retire. Do you honestly think you'll be healthy enough to enjoy the things you want to do now? Do you know how many people I've heard who have had work injuries, accidents, heart attacks, or any other stress-related illness before they reach retirement age? Three out of four!

Living your life around a job, rarely taking vacations, and living with low-grade stress and anxiety is not really living.

Why Start A Side Hustle

Why does anyone want to make more money? Maybe it's a need to make ends meet because the 'job' you have just won't cut it. Maybe you are building towards something more. Hell, maybe you're biting at the bit for something better.

You don't really need a reason. Just a drive to start something new. And just doing to make more money is a good enough reason. We don't need to be all altruistic about this. My first side hustle was because I was tired of my crazy hours. I had to get up at 3:30 am 5-6 days a week. Due to that job, I had no social life. Everyone else was getting home when I was going to bed. Passed out before the sun even set.

That was the time I really started looking into alternatives and found that there were options to working from home. Not gonna lie, my first forays in this were not very successful. I mean, the jobs out there really asked for too much for little pay. Also, I was not really in love with the idea of freelance writing.

But that was the Wild West years ago when all of this was so new. Especially, right when the bubble popped. I was in college and could see that what I originally planned to do was not going to happen. But it was all trial and error back then. You could find little pockets of people discussing this. Or help each other out to figure if something was a scam. (Now I sound like I'm old. "Back in my day..." I guess I could say I was really lucky to have my 20s to make all these mistakes and learn.)

And that's why I'm writing this for you now. To help you build a better foundation. A little less error. And resources that will help you a lot more. As there are too many people out there still telling us that we need to just choose one and stick with it. That we have to niche down and not stray.

I say screw that!

Yes, we are our Brands. But we are not only a brand. There are so many other things that do not fit into one Side Hustle (or Business). And sometimes, you want to be able to do more than one thing in your life. Who says you have to choose one?

Old wisdom and conventions still push people to get a job and have them "take care of you". But people forget that they are there to make money. And the bigger the company, the less likely they will care about your needs. They choose your health insurance, that you still pay for. A fixed income with extremely slow growth and very few options to move up. Plus the pressure to work outside your hours. But there are so many other options out there. And doing it alone isn't as hard as it used to be. Options for health insurance, doing your taxes, bookkeeping, and all the back-end.

Here are some of the other great benefits for having a side hustle (or several):

It can work around your schedule. You can make sure you are always off in time to pick up your kids. Always have Sundays off to laze around. You never have to get permission from a manager to take some time off. Since you'll know in advance you can get as much done before and either take a break or get someone else to take over for the time.

- It will always be something you enjoy doing. You get to decide what you do. And if you ever don't like it you can stop. Find another side hustle and move on.
- You are your main obstacle.
- There really isn't a cap on how much you can make (if all your hustles aren't service-based.)

The old model of working at one job until you retire is over. Ever since the 2008 Recession (a smaller movement before that), people have been moving around from different jobs. Not staying at places that don't satisfy them. Knowing they deserve better pay and actual sick leave. But the entrepreneur world has changed too. We don't have a lot of capital upfront to get started. You don't even need a physical store to sell from.

You don't have to stick to the same old boys club mentality or always pushing for the sale. Only working with big names, exchanging big money. You can make a decent living with normal people online. No weird gimmicks. Having to go to the office. Hell, a lot of things don't even need a suit anymore.

But I believe the next evolution has started. The idea that you don't have to be only one thing. That you don't only have to do ONE THING. That you can make a good living from several avenues, streams of income. That you do not have to hustle with all of them constantly to make money. That the hard and easy will have cycles. Hell, you can just do work on some for a short period of time.

THE GIG ECONOMY IS BOOMING

The quote "Money can't buy you happiness" is only partially true. Mostly because people take it the wrong way. It's supposed to mean an excessive amount won't give you money. Not that wanting and getting more can't lead to happiness. Just that it won't fill the giant void in your heart. Being able to take a vacation is not bad.

Because that will lead to less stress. No anxiety that you can make ends meet or be in big trouble if there was an emergency. Giving you the mental space to do more enjoyable things.

Now, what I'm giving you here is not a way to get filthy rich. (If you do, good on you.) But a way to get out of the poverty cycle. Even if you are not in it yet, you are a lot closer to it than you think. Can you just leave work for a week to help a family member with a medical emergency? Can you survive without a car in the long term? Can you afford to take several days off work and not get paid sick leave?

Most people answer "no" to these. Being gone from work for multiple days will not get you enough to pay your bills. Yes, you can just try to get a better paying job or get a raise at the one you got. But those are in a limited supply and again in someone else's hands to decide.

It is ultimately up to you how to arrive at full life (and bank account). It may be you only want a small hustle just to pay off some bills or save up for a down payment. That you only have it when something comes up. But others may want to double what they make without the added stress of management. Or, like me, you just want to do things differently and screw the rules.

Some of you may be getting frustrated at another thing to add to your to-do list. Like you aren't doing enough already. And I understand that you want less on your plate. But the idea behind a side hustle is that you will be able to create space and money for what you do want in life. You will get into the habit of making room to work on it and having less stress about whether or not you can afford the things you need.

People get stressed out feeling like they need to make huge changes to their lives, make millions, and reinvent the whole wheel to make big changes. You might not want to spend your whole life. You can be perfectly happy with most of it. But you do not have to keep only doing things that society deems as "acceptable".

You can start with just a few hours on your weekend to get started. Get up 30 minutes early in the morning to go through any messages you have. You can have most of your information up on a website or Facebook page with services/products, range of prices, and times you are available. Having the parameters and boundaries set up upfront will save you some headache. This also means at home. Maybe you get an hour every night to work on your hustle uninterrupted.

Those are others' made up rules and you do not have to try and be better at someone else's game. Be different. You're playing your own game. Your path will be different from everyone else's. But that doesn't mean that part of your path cannot intersect with a well-worn one. Or that you can't follow a guide for a while.

The majority of Americans graduate from high school. That is a well-worn path for all of us. One that many need to advance in life. However, our schools are different from state to state, district to district. I should know, I've moved at least a dozen times by the time I graduated. Almost every kid read The Great Gatsby, but each school read it at different times. Different grades and different parts of the year. Your school life could be different because of how your district was set up. The lines for the two junior highs in my city were completely different than the lines for the two high schools. Hell, my school bus drove past the other junior high to get to mine.

Each path is unique even with the well worth path of school. You still have different teachings and interactions. Your lived experience will be unique, even if you find people who have done almost the exact same thing as you. So, you feel like you're jumping on some bandwagon by starting a hustle. Or that you'll be doing something that already has so many people doing. So what?

Nothing we put out has to be 100% unique and original. I'm gonna leave that to the geniuses out there to find some new law of physics or invent teleportation. I have no aspirations for that. We've all been to the grocery store. How many varieties and companies make bread? How many different kinds of shampoo have you seen?

People buy them or they wouldn't be on the shelf. So there's space for them. Because as a species we need variety. My needs for shampoo will be different than most. I have long, straight hair, and not curly but I don't need anything to help with color since I don't dye it. Since I have a skin condition so I need a more natural option and I'm environmentally conscious so that's important too. The point is that what you do just needs to be different. No matter how many other options are out there.

What you do does not need to be so different to beat the rest. Your game, your rules. Just be different to what is important to you. Maybe your shampoo will be more neutral scents. Maybe you add biodegradable glitter. Maybe it's just where you source your ingredients locally. You just need to do the best for you and create a product or service that delivers what your people need.

My own path has been a winding, zigzag mess and I wouldn't have it any other way. Looking at each piece individually, you wouldn't think it was special or unique. How many people have a Liberal Arts degree? How many have worked in retail? The thousands of photographers there are just in my town alone? The millions of books written?

But when you put it all together, it is a path that no one could have followed. No one would have learned the things I have.

WANTING MORE MONEY IS NOT A BAD THING

Any of us starting a side hustle isn't new, unique, or innovative but how we do it or why can be. I hope millions of people start side hustles. Because for me, it's several steps towards freedom. And freedom means creativity. It means security. And ultimately it means choice. We all deserve more choices in our lives.

Choices on where you live and what you do with your life. Whether you stay in a job because you want to or because you have to pay bills. Getting out of the paycheck-to-paycheck cycle. Actually being able to afford to go on vacation, let alone go somewhere to relax. I knew we were not well off growing up because of the few vacations we took were always driving to visit family. Always staying with someone and never at a hotel. Rarely eating out, buying food to cook there. Everything was seen as extra.

We shouldn't have to live like that. Not saying we all need to take luxurious trips with villas and staff, but we are not meant to be working all the time. Always producing something for others.

There is still a prevalent belief that money is evil. That wanting it, wanting more, and enjoying it is morally wrong. Money is a tool. It's not good or bad in itself, but what you use it for. If you just want to live paycheck-to-paycheck that doesn't make you selfish. Wanting a bigger house so your kids can each have their own room is not believing you're better than others. You just want a better life for your family.

I don't know who put it in our heads that we can't take vacations. They should be kicked in the balls. Because everyone should travel. It opens our world and makes us more accepting.

This is what I want for you. Some breathing room. A chance to really live life in any capacity that you want. There is plenty of money out there. Your wants and needs do not take away from anyone else. So, making more money does not mean that others will make less.

I mean, there are people sitting on billions of dollars and no one is guilting them for having it. (Well, they should feel guilty because they could do so much good with it. Plus, the moral grounds of how they made the money are way too heavy for this book.)

You doing better makes others' lives better too.

Mindset

Running a side hustle (or several) is a very different thing than having a normal job. You are all used to getting in your set hours, coming home, and doing what you want. (Minus family obligations.) But you need to think about it very differently than you would regarding a hobby.

Yes, the 'side' part usually means that you do it around other work. But you cannot only do it around everything else in your life. You need to make time for it, most likely every day. There will be set tasks you have to do all the time. Scheduling and overall customer service.

I do want you to build these up so that you can run lite, on time, and effortlessly. But there is a lot of work you need in the beginning to get to that point. To make more than enough that you can take other things off your plate.

Though the "side" part is appealing because we all want to be able to make some income that takes less time and work than a regular job, so it cannot only take some of your attention.

Another part of mindset is getting around the "employee" mode that we all have been trained to do. Where we are trained to do a specific job, which is mostly just a part of the whole.

In a hustle, you are still running it as a business. Just a smaller scaled one. Where you are doing everything, and I mean everything. Most people will not have the means to hire help for most of what you do, not knowing what you will need. You will have to research, pick, and choose what you can have another do. This will only be contract work, usually one and done.

The rest is up to you. Sales, marketing, budgeting, customer service, legal documentation, design, just to name a few. Every decision is yours to make.

This is the point of starting where you get to decide what you do and how you do it. I am not bringing this up to freak you out but just prepare you for all the other work you will need to do.

A lot of people create a side hustle that is an offshoot from work they already do. You may feel great since you have so much of the expertise needed to get started. But you won't get the best out of this if you don't work on the other areas.

Even if you have specialized training or schooling for this specialty, there will still be gaps you need to fill. Yes, you are steps ahead, but you will not be able to put something together in an afternoon and hit go.

Another point to think about is not just to have a side hustle to make money. Yes, the point is to make money and create your freedom. I want you to think about the longevity of what you do.

If what you choose has a purpose for good, a purpose for the customer, it will last longer. Longer for you because it ties to something deeper. Longer for the customer because the service will be better when you are more invested in the outcome. Just because I have the time to babysit, and people would trust me more being a woman, I would not enjoy it. I would not do anything extra and would count the minutes until I could leave. That is not worth the money. The kids deserve someone who would want to be there and enjoy their company.

None of the options you choose should ever be a quick grab for money. Some of you may have some resistance to trying certain things because it doesn't "feel right" to make money from something that is easy for you, others give away for free, or are connected to charity or service.

But the other direction should not be true either. No one wants to be seen as that selfish person who wants to make cheap, defective products and sell them overpriced.

FREEDOM MINDSET

You can still make money and keep your integrity.

Follow your passion and the money will come. But if you love what you do/it's easy for you/ it's not essential, why can't you do it for free? Sounds frustrating? Oh, it gets worse.

Don't even get me started on 'the money will come'. That has almost never happened and I'm pretty sure most of those stories of all the time and effort went into what they were doing. You literally painting a picture will not get in front of anyone or market it in any way to sell it.

I can't even count the number of instances I've heard of people asking others to do things for free. Either they don't respect what you are doing or think it's not worth much. Think they deserve the "friends and family" discount. Think it won't take long so it's not a chargeable amount of time. Or the dreaded "exposure". (I cannot roll my eyes any harder.)

Just because it's easy for you to do doesn't mean it's not valuable. No one knows how much time you've taken to learn it. Whether or not you did it for years at a job. Expertise and speed should cost more. Why do you think people pay more for expedited shipping?

Or if anyone wants to do something of help then it should be like volunteering. Whether or not you do any philanthropy in your life, your hustle can make you money and help others. Doctors and Nurses get paid. EMTs get paid. It doesn't make you a bad person to expect the same thing too.

Now, I have seen a disproportionate amount of people in the wellness and metaphysical areas get pressured and told outright that they shouldn't make money for what they are doing. There is a belief that money is not important, the service is. But it gets pushed so far that any money you get from it can be considered "evil". (We'll unpack all that money stuff a little later.)

In every pagan, spiritual, metaphysical group/setting/gathering I've ever read or been a part of, there is always a discussion about whether or not to charge for what you do. How much you 'should' charge. They seem extra charged with whether anything is good or bad. Or, if you have any integrity for asking for money.

Money Mindset

Now, this is a big, deep topic and I won't be able to really dive into this, but it needs to be touched. Money is a part of everything we do. It's kind of the whole point of starting side hustles.

We all have baggage when it comes to money. Stories we carry from when we were kids. Stuff taught to us from our parents, family, community, and the world at large.

Whether it's your family who only works blue-collar jobs. 'Excess' money is for selfish, immoral, rich people. The only way to get ahead is to cheat. Our people don't do that. Or my personal favorite: women aren't good with money. There are these things that run at the back of our minds. Influencing everything we do.

I'm only going to go over a couple of things to get you started on working on this. They all come from Dennis Duffield-Thomas' book Get Rich, Lucky Bitch. So, if you really want to dive deep into this, I suggest going through her book.

As said above, the stories you live with need to be brought forward so they can be examined and released. Keeping them will not help with making more money, it will only sabotage you over and over. They are what people tell us or what we have seen. Not actually is true or even a part of who we are. These are blocks set up to protect yourself.

They protect you from what you do not know. Making sure you do not get hurt. One popular story is that money is evil. Only evil people have a lot of money. So you sabotage yourself from getting a raise or promotion. You spend everything you have so you won't be associated with it.

This exercise may take you several times to get the most out but you need to sit down and really dig deep for all the things you believe about money. Anything that you have any emotions for. That one Christmas you felt like everyone went cheap on your gifts. That one boss who made your first job hell and made you distrust ever working in a service job. Anything and everything, write it down.

There is no judgment on what comes out. You get to feel whatever you feel. We can't always control how we react to things, especially as children. Those emotions were just there to show you that something wasn't right.

There are other steps you can take with this but the other, huge one, is forgiveness. Forgiveness helps you to release these stories. Loosening their grip on your thoughts and actions.

"I forgive you. I'm sorry. I love you." Three simple sentences to start your forgiveness according to Denise. 'I'm sorry' to acknowledge whatever part you played. 'I love you' to truly push for the transformation. Not saying you love the person who might have wronged you. But more on a soul level, a blessing, to release.

You need to forgive the situation, the people in it, and yourself. Now, I know some people really don't like to forgive others. They feel like they are telling them that it was okay what they did to you and that they had every right to do so. But in the end, forgiveness is always for you. So, you do not have to carry the burden of emotions and memories.

But you also need to forgive yourself. For being in the situation. Whether or not you purposefully caused it. Forgive the fear, anger, and shame. It might have been a lesson you needed to learn. Maybe your energy level was what drew it to you.

And all of this does not mean you will ever forget. You shouldn't ever repeat it. You just need to release the energy that's holding this to you.

Now, I'm gonna be real, this will not be a quick and easy thing to do. You're gonna have to keep going back to that list and work on forgiveness over and over. Then when one clears, on to the next. Even after a while you're gonna need to check in that other stories haven't shown up. New things happen to you in life. Some of those will need forgiveness too. Honestly, it will probably be never-ending. Sometimes people and life suck but you do not have to let them hold on to you.

The Starving Artist

There is still the myth out there that anything artistic or creative you do will not make money. That if you go that route, you will ruin yourself and your family's lives and become homeless from it.

People are so dramatic.

It is a toxic notion that you will have to choose between food and art supplies, if any of your hustles go that way, this way of life is draining and will lead you down a path of unethical ways to make money. Even to the point where you will undervalue your work, just to get something.

Think about being more Andy Warhol instead of Van Gogh

It also comes from the idea that it's selfish to want to actually enjoy what you do to make a living. We all love to complain about our crap jobs, rude bosses, and awful commutes. Yes, there will always be something to complain about everything. But actually, having work that you enjoy and don't need a vacation from? Selfish.

When did it become a thing that not wanting to be miserable at work is asking for too much? Why is it bad to want more money just to buy fun things?

Anybody can make money off almost anything. It'll take a lot of work to do some of them, but it is possible. No one is laughing at the guy who sold pet rocks for millions of dollars.

On the other side, there's the notion that you are supposed to suffer for your art. Like it's noble and cool to do so. Or even that you have to do so to do any great work. That you can't create inspiring art, tell phenomenal stories, or do great work without suffering immensely for it.

Why would anyone do anything creative if you had to starve most of the time?

No one enjoys that and it's not healthy. Hell, it will shorten your life significantly. And why is that okay?

SCARCITY

The other part about money is the idea of what is or isn't out there. Our minds tell us that there's only so much to go around. Not enough good jobs out there. All the good guys are taken. Money doesn't grow on trees. So, your idea probably won't make much money. Are there too many out there like it?

There are trillions of dollars circulating out there right now. I have no time or space here to go over how so few people hold so much of the world's wealth. That anger needs to have its own book. You can have some of that.

People buy things they don't need all the time. A lot of great things out there are considered luxuries. Seeing what you have to offer may show people something they didn't know they wanted or needed. Giving yourself the space to be out there and allow others to see what your do allows abundance into your life.

You don't think you should try something because someone else is already doing it. So what? Have you looked at the cereal aisle at the grocery store? There is always more out there. There will be companies making and selling bread. Doesn't mean no one will buy it. You just need to have something unique that they want.

There are so many kinds for everyone's tastes and what you bring can always be shown to be different too. It can be just as simple as not being done by you.

Say that you want to be a photographer? Yes, there can be hundreds in your area. But you can break it down, depending on whether you do weddings, families, seniors, pets, journalism, sports, fashion, or dozens of other kinds. You can break those down into the style that you do. Light and airy, dark and moody, black and white, and the list goes on.

Even after all of that, there's the part where it's you. A

lot of people will work with photographers because they like them as a person. They like them on how well they give direction, make them comfortable, and take no crap. Part of the quality they want is what you can give them.

Yes, pricing will be a factor too. I'm not saying to stoop low so you can get more people. You need to price for the product and service you provide. We'll go over that in a later chapter.

YOU SHOULD BE GRATEFUL FOR WHAT YOU HAVE

Oh boy. This is a doozy. Now this line is true. We should always be grateful. Especially for all the good things in our lives.

But not when it's used to hold you back. I hear it too many times. That you shouldn't push for more. That wanting more or better in life makes you ungrateful. That it's black and white, wanting anything else instead of what you have means you don't appreciate it.

On another end, some want to shame you because they think you think you are better than them. Since they are OK (not happy) with where you are then you are looking down on them. That if so many others can live that way, you should too.

And you are not doing any of that. Their insecurities are none of your concern. You need to live your life how you need to. They can be perfectly happy where they are and you are perfectly in your right to not want to stay there.

We all need to stop having an aversion to being different. Just because it's something they've never heard of anyone doing or everyone around you only works blue-collared jobs doesn't make it bad. However, some people will never understand or want to.

You will have to decide how much their opinions matter. If they are close to you, then you might need to discuss this with them. But remember that this is their money story and they may not be ready to examine it. You may not get their support. You may have to find support somewhere else.

For people farther out of your circle, you may not convince them, even if you try. Most of the time you will have to ignore them. Why take advice from people who've never tried what you are doing and whose lives you don't want to live?

And you will get some snide remarks. Not many will believe you will make any money. That what you are doing will somehow rip the fabric of their society. That you are selfish for going in a different direction. You are not selfish. They just want you to feel guilty for nothing.

Plus, being selfish is not always a bad thing. We should stop being shamed for how we feel or the actions we take. Especially if they don't truly hurt anyone (if you really want to do any work on shame, you should really look at books by Brene Brown.)

Now, if you are setting new boundaries, not as available to work on your hustle or spending more time with your kids, to some that might feel awful. But that's because they could take advantage of your old boundaries.

HUSTLIN' ALL THE TIME

Now, this might be a little confusing. I'm all about side hustles and doing things differently to get your bread. But the idea of hustles was first about always working to get money. Always trying to get more, make more, have more.

And that's not the kind I'm talking about. That is the old school. Where every waking moment should be towards this.

My way is all about making things easier. Built for ease and aligned with what you want in life. Not to take over your life, but to make it better.

And this could just be in smaller ways of making it easier to save for certain things. Making your vacations a little extra special. Making sure you have a backup for actual disasters.

But it can also be bigger.

You want to be able to retire a few decades early (or at all). Pay off your house. Give you the space to leave that shit job that's barely keeping you afloat. You can start a business. Pay for several kids' colleges.

We need to get out of our heads the idea of always being busy. Like it's a badge of honor to never have any free time. It's not and I refuse to make myself feel guilty for not always being busy. The point is to not work so much so you can do the things you enjoy. Have the money to not worry about bills. Yeah, it can be a lot of work to have several hustles, but I will show you how to set them up where large chunks will work on their own.

Work smarter, not harder.

But I want you to build your hustle with intention and

that works for your life. That will fit into what time and energy you actually have to put into it. You can always find one that will fit.

Primarily because the way the world and economy are now is stacked against normal people. People who just want to pay their bills and enjoy some of their off time. But that's getting harder each year. Companies expect you to work more hours, sometimes off the clock. You can count on them to hit on you when something goes wrong.

Now, I'm not saying there aren't good places out there. But companies still need to make their money and there are too many places (honestly even just one is too much) that have no problem being unethical sometimes.

So, having something (or several) where you have the say or more power is helpful. You have something to fall back on if you need to leave your job or your spouse loses theirs. We all can use some added security in our lives and we need to be the ones creating it.

DOING SOMETHING THAT'S 'BENEATH' YOU

There is still this idea that there is work out there that should be 'beneath' you. That you only do as a teenager or until you get to 'better.

A lot of this is pushed by our parents. Which, rightly so, they want their kids to have a better life than what they had. They don't want a life of struggle for them. That they don't want to have to do back-breaking work and barely survive.

Or parents, family, and friends are already well off.

They are already doctors, lawyers, VPs at fortune 500s so you need to keep up with them. You have a standard to uphold.

This is all in the same vein that some work has little value. And that those people who work them don't either. That they can't be smart, good with money, and are lazy. And that job and this 'kind' of people don't deserve to earn decent money.

Firstly, that is just big businesses trying to make people think that so the latter won't have a problem with them paying these people crap. Then there's the scam that to not get stuck in those kinds of jobs you need a college degree. And we all know where that went.

If you work anywhere full-time you should be able to make a living wage doing it. That you should reasonably be able to pay for the basics on that alone. Shit, if you have a hundred employees but only the management can be full time, that company is cutting costs. They don't want to pay for any benefits and want control over how many hours people can get. So if they start making waves, there is always the threat of losing more hours.

A maid shouldn't get paid less for something you don't want to do. Hell, they should get more. You are willing to do something I dread, take my money. Y'all don't want to work picking up garbage or fast food. But those jobs are needed. Who else you think is gonna do it? It's not going to be only teenagers as a summer job.

So, if you have an idea for a side hustle that you don't mind doing, don't throw it aside just because it's not up to others' "standards". Don't go into it just because you think it's easy money. But if you don't think you'd mind doing it or even if you're just curious go for it.

Maybe you have an upper neighborhood nearby that your can do yard work for, or even scoop some dog poop. I have doing that and will pay to get that shit up (pun intended). There are enough people out there who will pay for quality.

SAVING MONEY/DO IT ALL YOURSELF

There is so much of the hustle mindset out there that's ridiculous. My side hustles, and what I'm trying to teach you, don't have you working every available moment. Doing it all because you can.

On one hand, many don't want to pay for something to be done for them because they want to save money. And I understand at the beginning, you will probably have to do everything yourself. But some people refuse to pay for something that you can "do yourself".

Yes, you want to make sure you understand every aspect of your hustle. You need to know how everything works. You will be doing everything yourself in the beginning but it shouldn't look like a noob did it all. But the saying "time is money" is actually true here.

You are paying for your own time. Time to do the things you are really good at. I saved myself at least a week of work having someone else do all my website copy for me. At that time, I took a few networking events and worked on my marketing.

It doesn't give you any added virtue to do it all. It

doesn't make me any more of a hard worker or more deserving of making more money. That's how businesses get big, make more money.

Scaling this way doesn't mean you need to be a multimillion-dollar conglomerate. You can just literally give someone else the job of marketing for you so you can spend time on the clients you have. But it took off five hours of work to your week.

And paying for another, to take things off your plate doesn't have to be so you can spend more time making money. It can be to take some stress off you. Just not have to do a task you hate. Hell, it can even be things you don't want to do in your personal time.

Hell, I'm building up so I can have someone come in and do all my deep cleaning in my home. Doesn't make me any less of a woman for not doing it.

People do care about appearances. At some point, if you want to make good money from your side hustles you need some professionals to help you out. Have someone make you a logo. I would have never known all the different files I needed. Or to make different variations and colors of it. Get professional photos done. Yeah, have good ones to put up on your website and profiles. But you need some that have more personality because people want to see the person behind the business. They can connect more with a person that they can relate to.

I know I've clicked away from sites that are too slow because its so crowded. The design in amateur or you can tell the logo was DIY. If you won't take the time to make things professional I'd be worried how well you'd do your job.

As Dennis has also said in her book (seriously go get her book), you are the golden goose. You are the one who is the center of everything. Even if you turn your hustle to have other employees, you are the one running the show. Why waste the time doing things that you actually don't like doing or someone else can do much better (and quicker)?

No, it's not counterintuitive to pay someone to do work you can do. How do you think I run all my side hustles? Different podcasts? Write books? Because the parts that I enjoy and what I make money with are the only things left for me to do.

Why be stuck with things I don't enjoy when I can get someone else to do it?

EMPLOYEE MINDSET

We have been trained since our school years to be employees. Forced, stringent work hours. Needing permission for most things outside work (needing permission to go to the bathroom or to go on field trips, and getting time off for vacations). Only care about efficiency. And you actually don't leave the drama in high school. You just have worse consequences for not fitting in.

And it will be hard to break free from this. It's been hammered into our heads forever. Plus, everyone around you will push for you to stay in the mold since that is the way everyone else is.

Not only do you need to value your time but a lot more.

Not only because you have to pay your own taxes but because you will be doing a specialty. No matter how easy it is for you.

At a job, you only do a small part of the whole. But going on your own, you are the face, marketing, supplier, and customer service. You have to pay for your equipment, maintenance, and everything inside the side hustle on top of your own salary.

I'll go over some ways to figure out some of this in the Pricing and Profit chapter. So, I won't bog you down with the math yet.

There is also getting over the idea of what you can do yourself, without permission. Or what time you need to work. Or how much time it should take you. A lot of people have a hard time getting over being paid really good money for something that takes you very little time.

That you don't only get paid in exchange for your time, like in a traditional job. But you are paid for your expertise. To save them time. For convenience.

Part of the problem with breaking away from the Employee Mindset is that others will not respect your time. If you are working from home, others will try to barge in on your work. Like it would just be easy for you to help them out quickly since you have time and at home.

On the other side, you do have time. You can take a Wednesday off to run errands. Or take a longer lunch. Get groceries in the middle of the day. You get to set your own schedule if what you set up allows it.

Now some of the things you build may have to work around customers. If you do lawn care, you can decide to only work four days out of the week. Maybe only take appointments in the morning. Or you do wedding makeup, so, only work on the weekends and only do the backend work on Mondays.

You will need to build up boundaries around your hustle. Many will not believe it's more than 'that cute hobby you do'. That you can drop what you're doing at any time to help them out. That having one week off means what you're doing isn't really important.

And you need to keep to those boundaries. Just because some of what you do can be moved around doesn't mean you should. Sure, pick up your sick kid, make room for that doctor's appointment, but don't go shopping with someone just because you can.

This is still where you make your money and should have the boundaries and respect of any job. By letting yourself be moved around to accommodate others you'll never get very far because it will always be pushed aside.

Going On Your Own Or Getting Help

When deciding what hustle(s) to choose, the first step is to decide whether or not to go in on your own or not. Each one has its own pros and cons with how much they can make, amount of work, and type of freedom.

If you're not quite comfortable enough to go about it alone, you can always find a hustle with a company or individual. Everyone knows about getting an actual part-time job at a store or restaurant. That has been the trend in this crap economy where too many of us can't really live on a regular full-time job.

Not gonna lie, this isn't my favorite option. It's good and good to get your foot in. To see what kind of money you want to make and what kind of time you actually want to spend on this.

But maybe you just don't want to do all the extra work in finding clients or customers and organizing everything. Sometimes you just want someone else to do a lot of the work.

No shame in letting others do the heavy crap.

These are great as a temp or seasonal jobs. Yeah, I'm trying to push this out as a stream. They are great for when your other streams take a dip. Or when you need a quick boost of income.

You could just do it part-time while you build up your other streams. Always good to have something constant until everything else gets running. It also helps with your taxes. But by letting them do some of the work, it takes away from your profits. You pay for the convenience.

You may also just want something like this just so you can get out and have interactions with people. Not all of your side hustles don't have to be working at home, alone.

So here's a shortlist of the pros and cons of working with a company:

Pro:

- You're already used to this structure.
- You can work part-time.
- They usually give some kind of perks (ie discounts, cheaper insurance, some paid meals).
- They pay the taxes for you.
- It can be fun since it's not a 'serious' full-time job.
- It gives you the time to work on other things.

Con:

- You still work on their schedule.
- They can change the hours you work.
- You're stuck at the same pay and very little chance to negotiate or get decent raises.
- Usually can't avail benefits.
- Stuck in the same work culture.
- HR really isn't your friend.

When it comes to getting something with a company you need to be always sure of what you need from it. You need to know if you just need a quick hit of cash or something that needs help for a longer time. What minimum payment you need. What kinds of hours and days you want to or can actually commit to it.

Yeah, when you first start out you may have to get a minimum wage job. Whether or not on top of your full-time job or in conjunction with building another side hustle. And for some, there will be a lot of resistance to do this.

I'm not going to go into all the implications about how any job should pay a living wage. Too much to dismantle, ain't no time, and off-topic. But there is a lot of belief out there that it's 'beneath real adults' to work those jobs. Any job out there should be respected and paid for fairly. You're gonna have to head back to the Mindset chapter to help work through this.

There will have to be some sacrifices. Never said this road wasn't going to be hard. You will have to figure out what you really want and how you're going to get there.

It may mean losing some of your free time until you can save up. Or take a cut from your income and lifestyle.

Though I love the idea of working for myself, it's not all sunshine and rainbows. Some people just prefer to not be completely in charge. Though I will always advocate using others so you can keep making money while you build up yourself, I don't want you to keep playing it safe. Or maybe having a part-time job around all the other side hustles just so you can get some people interaction and get out of your house.

Don't fall into the trap of staying where you know how things work. Never believing that you could build something (even small) on your own. Don't get trapped working somewhere where you are there most nights and weekends, away from your family. All this while the actual plan was you want to make more money so you could take more vacations with them. The money is less important if it literally fights against your ultimate goal.

Here are the pros and cons of going it on your own:

Pros:

- You are the boss and you get to make the decisions
- There is no cap on how much you can make.
- You can say no to whatever you want.
- You can choose your hours.
- There are a lot of ways to protect yourself.
- You know where all your money goes.

Cons:

- You are the boss, so you have to make all the decisions
- You can get stuck doing everything yourself (went over this in the Mindset chapter).
- No one else is to blame.
- No 'normal' hours.
- You are customer service and must battle the dreaded Karens.
- You have to figure out and pay all your taxes.

But there are other ways of just getting a part-time job. What I have moved more to are temporary jobs. There are a lot of opportunities (mostly in cities) to just do a job for a day to up to a week.

I have helped set up a Color Run and been one of the people to throw color powder on runners. Done ticketing for three weekends for a designer homes tour. There are hundreds of fairs and events every year that travel from city to city.

They pay more because they don't want to move all the workers they need for each event. Plus, you are a contract worker so you have to claim that income and pay taxes on it.

The way to find this is not easily known. It took me years to really get a good system done. A lot of these jobs are pretty physical, so be warned.

Some of the best places for these are online job boards like Indeed and even local ones (like JobsInMinneapolis.com or Indeed). You can even set it up that they send you updates for those kinds of jobs. Make sure that you are open to temp work and a little outside your area.

If you are not quite up to running something completely on your own but still want the freedom to choose what you do, you can always do freelance and contract work. This also works when you're not sure what direction you specifically want to go. It gives you the chance to try different things out.

You may not be ready (mentally or financially) to set up your own website and find clients. There are online marketplaces to set up shop. They give you the basic framework on what information you need to give, their terms and conditions, and some kind of fee (either up-front or per contract).

You can find different jobs right on the platform, though you will need to bid for each. But it is also a good place just to have if you go out of the platform to find clients.

These platforms give you some security. Payments are more secure. You don't have to give out personal information. There is someone else to go to if the client does not pay you or is harassing you.

But these markets are very saturated. It's hard to differentiate yourself. It's hard to outbid people who don't really care about doing this for more than fun money. Fees will eat at your profits.

Some of the big names out there right now are Fiverr and Upwork. (There are many others and I'll go over some more in Appendix II.) These places have a smorgasbord of contract work to get. They are also mostly for short or one-off jobs. Which can be good to get in the door and have something for your portfolio. There are some who use them to launch off their services. Turning those clients into recurring ones.

Etsy is the big site for products. Mostly what people know it for its handmade products, but there can be all kinds of products, physical and digital. For my business and hustles, I have had someone create a website template for me, design contracts, create stamps and stickers of logos, and design digital products. All from Etsy. There are so many other things you can make and sell on there. From jewelry, clothes, bags, costumes, household items, and even things you've upcycled.

Finding Ideas

There are so many different directions you can go for starting your first side hustle. Let alone whether or not you will run it on your own. And it can get overwhelming to think about what the "right" answer is.

In the end, there is no "right" answer. First, because I will help you work through your options and make sure you don't go into debt doing it. Two, even if you fail you can move on. You wouldn't have put too much skin in and you can learn from what didn't work. And three, this doesn't mean that you have to stick with it forever. You can move on whenever you feel like it. So you'll never 'waste' any of your other ideas. Plus, those other ideas can be in the 'not yet' pile. Nothing says you can't build up another side hustle once the first is rolling well. (Which is what I hope to help you get to).

Your side hustle can be an extension of what you already do. Someone who already does website or graphic design and designs some on the side. A teacher that tutors. Customer service works over many platforms. All of these can be done independently or you can work part-time or contract base through another company. You will just need to decide how much control you want in what work you do and how much you make.

A lot of my ideas have either fallen into or were thrown

into my face. But I didn't really start making money until I worked on the best ideas that were best for me. You might have an idea already that you think you could do. Remember, this doesn't have to be something big or take up a lot of time. The point is that you can fit it into your life and that it more than covers your cost and makes a profit. And that includes adding the cost of your time (we will go over how to calculate that in chapter 8).

A friend of mine Katrina Widener is an Entrepreneur Coach (which she is fabulous at) with three different revenue streams within her business. She does one-on-one coaching, group coaching, and has a workbook. Each with different price points, the amount of work that goes into it, and effort. The effort for her in what she gives the client and what the client does. Having different levels that people can buy from her.

While these all work great for her she also has something else on the side. She and two other friends decided to create something from their love of woo woo stuff. They created Show Me Your Woo, monthly events, and workshops covering all things woo. They wanted to learn more about these things themselves and knew so many others who did too but didn't know where to go. It was something they created that they found interesting. It doesn't take too much time since they all worked with their strengths within it. All from finding they had an interest in common. Then seeing the need out in the world and realizing they could be the ones to fill it. The only thing they had to pay for in the beginning was the website and venues they hosted at.

Sydney (who I've interviewed on my podcast) started out by teaching yoga. She did a lot of exploring after leaving her corporate job, and after going deeper into her spirituality she started learning and training in tarot and reiki. She takes on individual clients but she also teaches workshops, sometimes in collaboration with others. With the changing of times, she works on in-person offerings as well as online ones. Seeing what her community needed and asked for and figuring out how that fits into her business.

Just because people want something does not mean you have to fulfill it. You still need to have a sense of what you want to do in your hustle and what can fit into it reasonably.

When I first started Courageous Creativity I still didn't quite know what I was doing with it. I mostly was trying to figure out who I served, especially what I would be writing in my blog. It was around that time that I also started doing aerial.

Find three hobbies you love: one to make you money, one to keep you healthy, and one to keep you creative.

And once I really started getting into it, like most people, I wanted to fit in and have some of what most the others were wearing. And since aerial is part of the circus community, that means bright color and bold designs. But that also meant tiny sizes. Trying to find good legging that will hold with extreme stretch in bigger or even normal sizes left very few options.

This was just at the beginning of the athleisure trend so there were not as many options out there. And in my search I found posts and sites telling you how you could sell your own designs on clothes. So after a few weeks of really diving into this idea, I got my first legging designs. And I honestly didn't create them to sell.

I wanted something fun and colorful for myself and wanted to be able to make multiples so I could sell (at cost) to friends.

But something opens up in the universe when you take risks for yourself. One of the places I trained at kept seeing what I and several others were making. Found out they were mine and asked if they could sell some in their shop.

To say I was not prepared was an understatement. But I figured it out. I got more created and had my designs in their shop for over a year. I set up my own shop on my website. Expanding on other leggings, I added t-shirts, tanks, sweatshirts, and long sleeves.

Yeah, I could push for it to make more money. But I am happy that it pays for itself, my full website, and pays for someone to help me make the designs. It actually supplemented a lot of what I needed to really get started with my business.

I always advocate having a running list of side hustle ideas. And since I have such a love of paper products and pens I have a notebook specifically for this. I give each idea at least a page, to give enough room to put down enough information to be able to pick it up later.

Partially I do this so I always have ideas waiting for when I have the time and space to work on something new. When you have that kind of inspiration you don't want to waste time brainstorming the basics. But the other reason is so that you don't feel like you've wasted an idea.

So many people can't decide what to do because they think it means they're locked into that one thing. That they will never be able to explore that different idea/passion. But that's the beauty of side hustles. Since their nature is to start small, you can built-in other ones when you are able. And being small, you can also drop them whenever you want.

Finding ideas won't be hard once you know where and how to dig. The biggest thing you need to do is be open with yourself. The point of all of this is that you get to do something that you actually enjoy, make good money, and doesn't take a lot of time to do. So, you need to know what your likes and dislikes are.

DO AND DO NOT LIST

The first thing to make a list of is what you do, and do not want to be a part of your hustle. This can be something loose and short to start out. It will evolve as you go along. Either finding things you tried and do not want to ever do again. Or with this extra money has allowed you to let go of other things you don't want to do, parts that were associated with those could be okay with after.

When I first started out I wanted it to be creative and completely online. All the work I've been doing up to the point was in-person customer service. So the introvert in me really needed some alone time. And it was probably for the safety of the general public if I could get some time alone. Here was the first list:

- Online
- Create something
- Only spend 10 hours a week on it (I was already working 2 part-time jobs at that point so my schedule was all over the place)
- No coding or difficult computer work
- No set hours of the day
- I was in charge

That was it. Now that was great as it left a lot of things open, but it also left them a bit too open. So, I went to the next step to narrow things down. But having this list, which was added to a little later, gave me more parameters regarding what I wanted.

BRAINDUMP

This is the list you make of all the possible ideas of things you can do. This will take you several runs to get a good list going. There are some good questions you can ask yourself and others, and resources to look up more ideas. There are no right or wrong answers and no order, just possibilities.

There are plenty of questions to ask yourself to really start mining all that you can do. Most of us have felt like we have no particular skills in the beginning. But anything you do can be something that comes easy to you or really anyone. Plus, it can be one small thing. (Check out Appendix to see the example list I compiled.)

What's every little thing you've ever done for work? What have you or your co-workers complained about at your work that just doesn't work? What have your customers/clients talked about not liking or needing help with?

But also what have you been good at, in and out of work. Good with Word Docs or PowerPoint? Can organize a closet? Keep all your kids' schedule in order? Be able to calm down that one difficult customer?

There's a lot out there that you can freelance for with the work you already do. Or something that is hard to do at your work that you could find a solution for. Even if you worry about a conflict of interest, helping out customers on something they need help with can always be something that happens before they get to you at your job.

What things were you good at in school? What did you and your friends like to do? What did your friends always come to you for?

What do you like doing now? What are your hobbies? What are some things that would make your life or your life easier now? What are some things that you've always had an interest in? Something you've always wanted to try?

What are some things that your friends and family complain about now? What are your managers and bosses worried about getting done?

There should be no emotions when you make this list. No worrying about how to do anything. This is just to get your brain rolling in seeing all the possibilities. I also wouldn't worry too much about crossing anything off that doesn't appeal to you, we'll work on narrowing down the list later.

RESEARCH

Now it's time to search through what others have done. Lucky for you now there are a lot of places to search to get started. The easiest is just to do a search only. But it can be hard in the beginning when you don't know where to start. Since I've been in the game a while I've seen all of them. Some of the keywords you can search for are side hustle, work from home, freelance work, gig work, and really any combination of these.

This will bring up plenty of articles to get you an overview. And sometimes they give you some good ideas. But this will also bring up other websites that are specific to these topics. You can even find great Pinterest boards dedicated just to this. (I got one too @courage_create called Create Your Freedom.)

TO HOBBY OR NOT

A lot of people turn hobbies that they were able to make money on into a hustle. It can be a good idea. You already have the skill and set-up. It won't take much to push it to the next level. Some people can put more stringent parameters to their hobbies

The problem you can run into with hobbies is they

usually with creativity. For some, the extra pressure can dampen if not kill their creativity. You may only be able to do it a very limited time or in spurts just to not kill the joy of it. For some having timelines can be too much.

WHAT DO PEOPLE ACTUALLY WANT/NEED

We can all dream all we want about having a striving art studio or a boutique, but if you live in a small town of mostly farmers you won't get the traffic you need. Now that's not to say you can't change parts of it to fit your circumstances. For a season I sold clothes that others and I wanted to get rid of on eBay. Some people didn't want to drive to someplace to donate it or sell it themselves. So, I did it for them. For the people that didn't outright give me the clothes (got a bunch from a couple of hoarders who finally were cleaning out), I took 50%. Since I was doing the corresponding and shipping (plus taxes), they were just happy to get something back to buy other things.

I also started my own apparel line. Started off with cool and funny saying tops. Once the drop shipping company I used expanded what they offered, so did I. I got a lot more sales with my fun and funky leggings. To this day my apparel pays for itself, my websites, and all my domains. And that's all I want from this. I have fun with designing, most of which I wear myself, and it covers itself and a few other things.

WHAT ARE THE COSTS

You need to figure out what the costs are for running each idea. What will it take to start it and keep it going? Will you need to get supplies and inventory? Can you start off with just social media and an email? What is the last possible moment that you need to get a website, or upgrade, outside help?

Never go into a hustle blind. Just because you have interest from possible customers doesn't mean it'll be easy. Having an idea of what is required will help you from making mistakes and looking unprofessional.

You don't need to know everything, but if you don't know enough then there will be some costly mistakes. Do the research and have a rough plan. Know what you are going into and not just let the daydream take over.

THERE DOESN'T NEED TO BE A HIGHER CALLING

Whatever you choose does not have to be something bigger than yourself. Yeah, a lot of us want to do something because it helps others, we're good at, or it's challenging. But some things you just do because it looks fun.

One summer I decided to sign up for fun runs and obstacle courses. And not to run. I don't run. But I'd get there way before dawn to help set up registration, check people in, set up the course, and even be a part of the fun. The Color Run had to be my favorite. I got to be one of the people who threw the color powder on runners. Felt lucky to get the only section with two colors, peach and yellow. You got creative after a while on how to throw it. It was such high energy for hours, which most of my family thought was weird for me to go for since I'm such an introvert. It was so much fun and I sneezed color for a week.

In the beginning, or whenever you feel like it, you can just use a service that can you temp jobs or work-from-home. One of the best ones I still use is the Rat Race Rebellion email list.

But on the other side, you should just be doing it to make money. Not in the 'I need to make money to pay the bills this month', that's perfectly fine. We've all taken jobs that sucked but paid well. More than you should be doing something just because it can make you a lot of money, possibly quick. Especially if you have no integrity in it. Don't be making a crappy knock-off of something popular at the moment and not care that it has crap quality. Then close it down once it's not popular, ignoring all the complaints.

Doing something just to make money is not a bad thing. Money is just a means. But you need to actually care about what you are doing. What you do or make should help people and truly deliver their needs. Whether or not your hustle will be long term. You should always give quality. Then you're just a scammer taking people's money.

IN-PERSON VS ONLINE

The internet has opened up the world for all of us. With information, communication, and selling. What hustle you decide on depends on whether or not your business is online.

It can be exclusively online, or local, or a combination of the two. You could have the option to buy on your site but you mostly sell at farmer's markets. You can do coaching for anyone in the world with all the free options for video chat, but do group coaching twice a year at a local co-working space.

The possibilities are endless. Which can be part of your problem.

Of course, there may not be a need to choose depending on what you want to do. If you're planning and planting gardens, then you really need to be there in person. But really anything that you do should have an online presence.

With how things are now everyone searches and gets recommendations online. Even if you don't get a website at first (or ever) you still need an email and social media. Some hustles and businesses I've seen have only had social media to give out information and to give a glimpse inside. People need to be able to find you and you to be able to show what you can do.

Some people even just sell or do freelance work through an online marketplace. But the higher the traffic or price points, the more you will need a website. If not for the extra needed security but also for a central place people can go for more info. Plus you need to have a place just for your clients and customers, and all the legal stuff to cover your butts.

So, even though you need to have a presence online that doesn't mean you have to work online. You may want to have what you do be outside since everything else you do is indoors.

I always noticed, when running multiple side hustles, having at least one that requires being around people. Even being an introvert I couldn't do everything alone. Partially to just get out of the house and get out of the same area, but just to keep up with talking with people. It's with being out that I can get my creative juices going. Hell, there were times working with customers that I got new ideas for other side hustles. Enough people complain about things. Not even about where you are and what you are doing, just something in their life.

Don't get me wrong, I love being able to work from home, make my own schedule, and take breaks whenever I want. But sometimes I need to be reminded that there are other people and how to interact with them.

You can even have different side hustles that are with people and outside only be seasonal. Working the Renaissance Festive for only 6-7 weeks is great fun. It's busy, I get to wear fun costumes, and I can get tipped for being weird. But it's also a lot of people, hot and dirty. I always love doing it, but I'm happy when it's over.

Now some of the other people who work there follow the circuit. Where they go from one festival to another. Either as performers, sell their products, or do a service for sometimes 10 months out of the year. That's how they want to make their money and they can handle that kind of schedule. I could not. Doing the one in my state is enough for me.

I even worked at a snow tubing place over the winter.

Which paid very well for our Minnesota winters and I was lucky it wasn't a horrible frigid year. Was just in the mood to work outside at that time. While the next year, I worked at a greenhouse for a summer. Not gonna lie, I loved working at both but the extremes in temps were definitely something I could not do all the time. That's the best part of these. You can do them for a short time and let them go.

TIME AND ENERGY

When you go through all your ideas of what hustles you want to try you will need to keep in mind what time you have if you are going to need to be somewhere physically. Or if you only have late evenings to work on it then you may need to keep it online.

I always recommend doing a mixture of things online and out in the world. Whatever ratio you choose is up to you, mostly depending on your temperament and lifestyle. Me, being an introvert, I only do in-person things every once in a while or in spurts. Or maybe you have them for your seasons like you do more things from home right after the holidays until the spring. But you love to do pop-up shops all summer long.

You will have to figure out what time and energy you have to whatever side hustles. Plus figure out how they change throughout the year. Your family has its own seasons where they are busy together and individually.

Active vs Passive

What I mean by Active is something you do in exchange for money that has a time limit. Mowing someone's lawn, cutting hair, or designing a website. There's a set time to do the work, you get paid for that amount of time, and you really can't be doing other work at the same time.

It's the equivalent of having a regular job.

There is a lot of buzz out there about creating Passive Income. And the idea is great because you can do the work upfront and keep getting sales (supposedly) forever after.

It is a product (digital, paper, ecourse, etc) that you create and send out into the world. Just kidding, there's a little more to it.

Say you have a coaching business. You enjoy doing your one-on-one with clients. But to bring up your income you raise prices and create a group coaching program that you do 2x a year. That creates less work for you and a lower price point for your customers.

But to create passive income you create a workbook that illustrates the first two steps that all your clients go through. Or you could create an e-course that is the basics of what your clients go through in the first 3 sessions with you.

This is one way you can add income streams to one Hustle.

You could also just have one that is only e-courses, selling digital photography, printables, and dozens of others. It could literally be about something you are good at. Does not have to be connected to your work or any other Hustle.

But a lot of people usually start out with what they already are great at.

Maybe you love building computers, but don't want to actually build them for others. But you can create videos that walk you through how to build your own. Have some PDFs with the recommended parts and equipment. Get some sponsors for your videos that relate to what you make.

A lot of coaches out there do this very well. Of course, they have their one-on-one services. Then they branch out to having group coaching programs. Then they create an e-course about some of the topics they go over in their coaching. Plus they have different workbooks and guides.

On one side, this is great because it gives different price points for people to get into. You really need different levels to capture more clients/customers. (We'll talk about not being for 'everyone' more in the marketing chapter) giving them a point that is comfortable for them to work with you.

You will have plenty of free info out there (well, you should by the time you launch whether it's blog posts, guest posts, podcasts, video channel, or social media) that lets them get to know you. And some people are never comfortable paying big bucks for things right away. They need to build up their trust in you. While there are others who are your biggest bang now.

On the other hand, you need different levels because some people just want a different option. Some people want to have their hands held or even have things completely taken out of their hands. Others want the info so they can do it themselves. Or they want to see if what you give at the bottom will be worth their time before they take the dive with the big bucks.

ACTIVE

What I mean by active is something you have to do each time to get paid. This is the one that's the closest to what you're used to at a job. You get paid for your time. Whether it's a project that you do or something you create that you need to sell at a farmer's market.

These are for the people who want to interact with people more, either online or in person. You don't do any work unless someone wants it.

Some may need to have work that requires more routine. Just slightly different per each customer or client. Whether it's planning a wedding or fixing up cars. They like to have a project that has a beginning and an end date.

Now, most people start with this option. There is very little upfront cost and no training. Since they usually are using a skill they already have.

Services

This is usually the first thing people think of when someone starts something new. Especially when you're young.

A paper route and babysitting to working part-time at a restaurant. It's pretty self-explanatory. You do something for a customer, you get paid, and done.

Products

Now, most would think this would all be passive but if you make things that are personalized or customized you have to make them per person. These can be things like creating an astrological chart, custom artwork, or an audit. This is also taking pictures for a wedding, designing a website for someone, or creating a doll to look like a child.

PASSIVE

Passive income is something you make once and can be sold over and over again. Writing a book, selling a stock photo, or really any digital product falls into this. Though there are a lot more options out there for dropshipping, so products fall into this too where a secondary company will make your product for you (for a cost) when someone orders it.

It gets made usually before you put it out into the world. Although you can do a presale or something like a Kickstarter to get money upfront and to be sure what you're making is viable. But most of the work of making is in the beginning.

Now 'passive' is a little misleading. You can't just make it and send it off into the world and expect to make money from it. None of us has Oprah status. You still need to do marketing for it every once in a while. Share it in your email list or post it to your social media.

Actually, you need to do a little research (like with this whole thing) to make sure you have a market for what you are making. Because anything passive cannot be a service. You need to see what the need is out there for what you want to make.

Physical Products

You can actually have a passive income from physical products. There are so many more options out there now than there were even five years ago. I'll give an overview of them here but if you want to see all of them specifically check out Appendix II.

Say you are a photographer. Yes, you can do weddings or portraits. But you also have the option of selling some of your photos as Stock Photos or even dropship the printing of your photos.

Stock photos have different needs than what most people want hanging on their walls. Though this is more of a long game than a quick way to get money. You need to have a huge inventory and it can take some time to really figure out what people are looking for. But after a while, you can really make some good money.

Now, if you want to take more artsy photos setting up a website where people can order prints might be up your alley. These can be canvas, print of wood, print of metal, card stock, postcards, or even framed. If you really want to go out there you can also print on pillows, blankets, phone cases, mouse pads, and a whole bunch of others. It just depends on what kind of brand you want to portray. Someone who wants to be seen as more serious and classy may want it to look its best which would be on a normal canvas or paper and not a pillow.

Of course, with anything to do with photography, you need to have the right contracts. If there are any people in the image, it doesn't matter if it's their back and you can't reasonably recognize them, you still need a model release form. If an image was taken at an event while you were working, but there are no discerning things in there to recognize, you still need permission from the people running to use it.

If you are an artist and even just like to design things, there are more things you can dropship with. If you don't need much depth and detail you can always print on a post, t-shirt, tanks, sweatshirts, leggings, hats, stickers, and swimsuits. There are probably other options I'm missing because so many new things keep launching.

If the written word is more your thing you can also work on journals and books. Everyone knows about e-books, but few know that even though Amazon and Barnes and Noble you can set up Print On Demand.

With anything you do with dropshipping, you will not get as much of a profit from it. Since they have to have the product, print it, and ship it for you they take a huge chunk. But most sites let you choose what price you sell at. You'll have to do the research on what would be a good price for your customers and what profit you would need to make it worth it.

Digital Products

If you do any searching online it's easy to find examples about doing digital products. They are the usual options people see. These are PDFs, printables, images (this also includes photos), music, audio, video, and really anything you can just get online.

For the most part, they are easier to make because there isn't as much formatting you need to do.

Figuring out where to see is another thing you need to take into account. It's always good to have your own website. It's the space that you own and you don't have to pay anything extra (minus what the website costs). It's always good to have a site just so you have someplace to direct everyone to. For all the things you offer, more information about you / your hustle, and just anything else you think is important. Overall building trust for your brand.

Marketplaces are a good place to start out. It's already built-in with all the tools you need to get started. They usually have tutorials about all the things you need to get set up, marketing, and ideas about what people are looking for.

Some of the best digital products you can sell are stock photos, templates, website themes, printables, and designs. There are literally a hundred things you can sell digitally. You just make them once and be able to re-sell them over and over.

Marketing

Once you get your Hustle up and running the other half of the battle is getting the word out there. You need customers to make that bank. And marketing is just as important as your product/service.

First, you need someplace central for people to find you. If you can have a physical location, that's good. Even if it's the same area at the farmers' market every weekend that people know to find you. Your hustle may not be in person so this may not be necessary.

But what is a website?? Someplace people can search for and find all the information they need. What you do, ordering, scheduling, calling/emailing, and any other little detail. It's the one place you can send people for a lot of their questions.

A website and email (will get to that below) are your property. Your space doesn't change unless you do it. All the others, especially social media, is rented space. You have no control over the algorithms, banning, and any other policies they put up. Now, they are great and should be used. But they need to point towards what's yours.

WEBSITE

There are a lot of free options out there to get started. But if you really want to look professional, you will want to buy your own domain (the actual URL). I'm going to give a few good options that I have tried, give pros and cons, and the costs to them. I'll throw in some places that you can buy a domain in the Appendix II. Of course, there are a lot more options for hosting your site but these are three main places most people go to.

Squarespace

This is what I use right now and have been with the longest. It has the easiest drag and drop options but still gives a lot of options for customizing. Their customer service is very good and they have an extensive library that answers many of your questions. What I love about those is that they not only have the info written out, but there is almost always a video showing how to do things. Plus, if you don't find exactly what you are looking for, they link you to the forum with related topics on the page.

Wix

I've seen this mostly used for photographers as it is very photo-heavy. It is the same idea as Squarespace in that there is a lot of drag and drop. This is the cheaper option but it also has lesser features. But for something basic, this will give you all you need.

WordPress.com and WordPress.org

Now this will be slightly confusing. WordPress.com is the free option but you do not get a secure and custom domain. It will be 'name'.wordpress.com and for some people that may be just fine. But if you want to seem more professional and legitimate, you're going to need a domain that you own.

WordPress.org is the host when you have a domain. This is the big place you want to be if you really want full customization. It is great if you want that to show in your branding. But if you don't have much experience with coding or can pay someone to do it for you, you will be stuck doing the basic stuff.

I started out with WordPress. I liked using it, even though I mostly blogged in the beginning. I could figure out most of the stuff I needed at the beginning by myself. But after a while, it got a bit tiring doing all the searching trying to figure out how to do each new thing. Not saying I didn't like learning it all but I just didn't have the time for all the things I wanted to do.

REFERRALS

The best way to get new customers has always been from a referral. People believe in a product and service more when there is an actual person recommending it.

In the beginning, this may only be your friends and family. Which is fine. Just make sure they have the right info and actually know what the hell you do. It's funny, and sometimes disheartening when someone shares something that has nothing to do with what you do, how much it costs, or what kind of turnaround you have.

And make sure if you do work for them you let them know whether or not you gave a family discount or not (upfront) and not to go telling other people about it. We will discuss this more in the Pricing and Profit chapter but you need to figure out before you get started whether or not you will give discounts in the beginning.

Referrals can be set up where people you can give a code to certain customers that they can share with people. Whether it's a link so you can see what kind of traffic they drive to you and you give them a gift. Or even a discount for anyone they share to use.

After every time someone buys from you, give them a couple of options to share and give you feedback. This does not mean all of them in the immediate email you send. Maybe in the slip, your ship to them or the email, give them some of the places they can share what they bought. Then a week or so later, ask them how they are liking what they got or the service.

You can ask them to go to your site, fill out a form, or a site that does reviews and ask them to leave a review there. I prefer to have them either email me back or fill out a quick form. First, so if there is a problem you can handle it privately, and quickly since it goes straight to you. You can also edit some things before putting them up. Not outright lie about what they said but maybe rearrange it to show you answering their question. Or only using a small part of it if it's really long.

Make sure you have all your social media set so people

can tag you when they talk about your product or service. Plus, you can repost them on your own and even save what they wrote, along with the image (if available) to use in other places for your marketing.

It's always in good form to ask for permission before doing this. Yes, it is up on a public social media site, but there are still copywriter laws. And you don't want to get bad press just because you didn't ask first.

EMAIL

Having an email dedicated to your particular endeavor is an easy way to stay organized. Especially if you have more than one. Just as you have a different work email to your personal one, you want to keep things separate. You do not want an inquiry to get lost in all the other emails that come in throughout the day. Or get a bad review because you didn't see it soon enough to fix a problem.

Luckily now, things have relaxed so you can just have a Gmail email with your business name in it and most people won't bat an eye. If you build it up enough, you may want to get one that's more specific but it's not necessary anymore.

The biggest thing when it comes to marketing is having an email list. Again, this is your ownership. People sign up to hear from you and you go straight into their inbox. Which is what you need a service like this for. Not just to send an email to everyone but different pages for signing up for your email list. Not like social media where if people are not on until hours after you post they never see it. You can have different sign ups on every page on your website and even put links on your social media.

As with websites, there are some good free options like MailChimp and Mailerlite being the main ones. These have the least amount of customization to them. Which for some, you don't want any extra branding and all the bells and whistles. Just something to send out the info you need, some links, and maybe an image.

Convertkit now has a free option as well. All of them are free for up to 1,000 subscribers. This gives you a bit more that you add to your emails. Add a logo or even create templates. I like this because you can create different triggers. If someone signs up for one thing (a free worksheet on your site), it triggers that another email sequence will get sent to them over time automatically. You can even divide people into different categories so someone who supports your podcast won't get anything about your apparel line.

Now, what you do with your list is up to you. Same with any business you signed up for or ordered anything from, they will send promotions. You can send when you are going to be at an event or even a blog post you wrote. Everything still leads back to you and your hustle.

SOCIAL MEDIA

Social media is free and can be a great tool. But a point to remember: it is only rented space. Algorithms change all the time. And at any point, they can kick you out or completely shut down.

But it is a great space when it's working. You reach so many more people than you could ever do in person.

I'm mostly going to talk about the giants in the arena right now. There are so many other options out there where your demographic hangs. I will touch a bit on some of the others I've seen working and how others have used them. But the landscape is ever-changing online and I'd rather give you what you need that will last a while than something that will only be here for a season.

Even if you don't use but a couple of these, it's always a good idea to get on all of them and get your name. Don't want anyone else taking it as a chance to confuse people about whether or not it's connected to you.

Facebook

I'm sure you're not surprised with this being here. Facebook is a juggernaut that you really cannot afford to not have a presence there. Even if you think it's "too old" for who you serve. One reason you want to be on here, even if your customers are a lot younger. Most will be on here because everyone else is on it. They want to make sure they have their own personal one. And a lot of them may only get on to connect to relatives.

Second, their parents will be here. And if your customers are young they may not have their own money, or even need permission to get something like what you offer. They may even ask for it as a gift. If you can be shown as a 'real' business on Facebook, they will be more likely to trust you.

Third, even if they don't do anything there, they usually need something to connect to Instagram. If you want to have a business account on Instagram, you need to have at least a business page on Facebook. They have to be connected since Facebook owns Instagram. It is its own platform that nothing else compares to. It is set up for people to connect in their everyday lives but also to make connections with groups. These groups can just be for fun and mom advice, all the way to building businesses.

Instagram

This is another beast in itself. Different setup and demographic. While Facebook is a little older, Instagram is more for the Millennials and those who are a little younger. And it is image- and video-heavy. With so many new updates, I will not be going into too much detail since by the time this book comes out, there will probably be another algorithm change and new feature updated.

Not only do you have your feed to post but Instagram now has Stories (to compete with Snapchat), IGTV (against YouTube), and Reels (like TikTok). These are all slightly different things. Mostly pushing for more videos because many believe that is the direction social media is going. They may not be wrong, but I won't be making any predictions. Just following what I need and throwing out the rest.

Youtube

YouTube started a year after Facebook. While it may not be classically categorized as a social media platform, it still has a place for you to use for marketing. In the beginning, this was where you could upload long forms of videos (or short).

Some people build full brands and businesses on here. Doing funny videos, how-to's, tutorials, and everything in between. Yes, you can use it to build up your business but you can also get money from this platform on its own. All the other platforms did not have this built-in at the beginning with ads.

TikTok

This is the new game in town, for now. Honestly, things change so fast that the next new thing could come up any day now. These are 15 second or less videos that's a fun distraction for a short or long time. This is great to show behind the scenes and your fun/funny side.

Snapchat

This is used mostly with the mid-20s and under. This is another quick use app. People can use it for a few minutes or for hours. Many use it for fun, silly, entertainment.

It reaches about 11% of the digital community. Geofilters help promote local audience engagement. Brands can create art graphics that appear over Snaps when users are in a specific location.

LinkedIn

This is more like the professional's Facebook. You pretty much have your whole resume on there, make connections, and can post things to your wall. But it's all supposed to be to a higher standard. It also gives you more credibility to your brand.

Twitter

If you are a wordsmith, then this might be the place for you. However, it seems to work a lot more for those who are not heavily image-based. Sharing articles and general thoughts.

Pinterest

Though this is technically a social media site, it doesn't really act like one. It's more of a search engine, only in images. Not gonna lie, I search here first before Google if I'm looking for something specific. Whether it's information, data, fashion, or just cute dog videos. Each image (and video) has a title and description that is easier to search for and they can be put into categories.

This site is a little less personal, you don't really write much in it. But pretty much anything that can be shared in an image or graphic can be shared here.

PHYSICAL FLYERS

Sometimes just throwing your one offer up on a flyer can

be enough to get the ball rolling. You can be mowing lawns and put up signs on street corners and in local businesses.

Or if you have something that's around an event or specific days, flyers work great. Something that only needs a few good details and nice bright color. Mostly because you have to worry about it staying up long enough.

If you need to have the information out for long periods of time, you need to budget in time and money to go back up to repost things. Or to replace damaged or dirty looking flyers.

NETWORKING / IN PERSON

There is the tried and true way and that is to just talk to people. Actually to their face. Have a short description of what you do so it is easy for people to remember and look up. And it needs to be short. If the person asks more questions, then go ahead and talk about it more. But do not be that person who just goes around being a talking advertisement.

Whether it is just out in the world or an event, you are not just there to talk about yourself. You are also there to talk and make connections. Most people will like you and remember you in a good light if you have genuine conversations. Find ways to make connections and be generally helpful.

GUESTING

Another good way is to get a signal boost from another's

following. This can be interviewed on a podcast, writing a guest blog post, or doing an Instagram takeover, among other things. It's great because you can get in front of another group of people. They usually do most of the work and try to make you look good.

Now, the main point of these is that you are giving a lot of good value in doing this. Whether it's pointers, advice, or even just a good story. You need to have something good to offer them and their audience.

DON'T BE A SPAMMER

Don't be annoying. There is a time and place to put up your information, especially online. All of these places are to be used to showcase what you do but it is not about you. This can be confusing since you are supposed to show who you are and give people a face for what you do, but not to make everything about you and your life.

Nobody likes that annoying person who friends you on Facebook or follows you on Instagram and very quickly DMs you wanting to talk about a great opportunity or product. Trying to get you to sign up with them. Get away with that MLM pyramid shit. (Don't come at me, it is shit and nothing anyone can say will change my mind.)

Another great way to be on people's mind is to be a good promoter of other businesses. Reciprocate whenever you can. Give reviews for anything you consume. Share it on social media and tag them, telling people why you like them. Think of it as a pay-it-forward. But don't be expecting people to reciprocate right after you do this. That's not what it is about.

Part of it can be good karma by supporting other businesses (preferably small), but it also shows others that you have integrity. It is leading by example. Plus, if you show your own customers and clients this, they are more likely to do the same for you and other businesses.

How to Price Your Work & Make A Profit

Figuring out what price you're going to charge is a sticky thing to do. Being new, you won't really know what things cost and what the average is in your area. But you will also have to fight against yourself.

I see it all the time. People undercharge because they are new. They don't have the 'necessary' qualifications. Or they're not an expert. There are a lot of excuses out there that people make. But you need to remember, you are here to be of service to people, and you can't do that if you can't make money from this. If you can't keep the hustle afloat, then you can't keep it up.

It's important to note that the quality of your work will set the tone for how you price your time, as cheap work attracts cheap clients. If you are creating a product that is high-quality, your clients will value spending the money to receive something higher-end.

Now that doesn't mean there won't be people who will try to haggle with you and not want to pay your prices. You're gonna have to get over the hurt feelings of that. Cause it's gonna suck. They will not value what you do for whatever reason; they don't think it's important, what you're doing is a "real" business, they could 'do it themselves', or they found it cheaper somewhere else. You need to stand strong for what you know you are giving.

Big does not equal success the same as small doesn't mean a failure.

Selling a Product: Time + Material + Overhead = Cost of Creation

When selling a product, it is pretty straightforward to calculate the cost of making that product and creating a well-priced item. To do that, you need to work through these three areas: the materials you use, your time spent making the product, and your overhead costs.

Raw materials: raw materials consist of everything you need to create or build your product (eg. ink, pens, and paper for calligraphy) plus the cost of packaging it (eg. boxes, postage, shipping, wrapping paper).

Time/labor: You have to pay yourself for your work! Your "labor" is the time spent making the product times your hourly wage. Paying yourself now for your time will help you price your product(s) right so that in the future if you hire employees, part of their salary will already be included in the product's price.

Overhead: Overhead is a fancy word for all of the expenses that you incur each month to create your product. These can include studio rent, insurance, design software, utilities, etc. If the expense is related to your product creation, it needs to be accounted for. Remember, when calculating your overhead, only include the expenses that are related to your product creation (marketing, sales, and advertising expenses aren't directly related to creating your product). Your marketing budget comes from your sales (or a loan, etc.).

Example: If you're creating and selling 500 clay pots a month, you'd calculate the material costs for those 500 pots (clay, shipping, etc.), plus the overhead from one month (rent of studio, etc.), plus the amount of money you want to pay yourself for making those pots. Then divide that number by 500 and you have a rough estimate of how much to sell each pot for.

Selling a Service: Time + Effort + Expertise = Cost of Service

Pricing a service is a bit more abstract than pricing a product, so the formula looks a little different. The cost of a service can also vary greatly, depending on each individual sale (eg. the cost of walking a dog that is dropped off at your home will be different than if you have to pick up the dog, take them to the vet, etc.).

HOW TO PRICE YOUR TIME

There are several different ways to approach creating your rate including hourly rate, flat rate, and income-based. A few things to keep in mind when mentioning profit (also known as net income): Profit margin measures how much profit your products/services/business makes, expressed in a percentage. If your profit margin is 20%, that means that

20% of the money you make stays in your business and isn't needed to cover expenses.

Hourly Rate

When you use an hourly rate, you track the hours you put in during a project and then charge the client for the total time spent working. While this is the most straightforward option, the pricing isn't always fair to us creatives. The great Paula Scher said it best: "It took me a few seconds to draw it, but it took me 34 years to learn how to draw it in a few seconds." Just because you're able to work quickly or do something in a short amount of time doesn't mean it should be cheaper for the client.

Now, this is where most people start. It's the easiest to start with. Especially where you're starting small you don't know what you don't know. And it's a lot of trial and error. No matter what you will under-price yourself. Either not knowing what you can charge, cause all you've seen were cheap options at big box stores. Or you will undervalue yourself whether you think it's too easy and that you shouldn't make X amount of money from it.

Flat Rate

Using this approach, you charge the client a single price for the entire project. You can create the price however you like, but it's usually based on an estimate of how many hours you'll spend on the project that times your hourly rate. This was the first approach I used. I estimated that a branding project would take me about 30 hours and my hourly rate was $25/hour. 30 hours x $25 = around $740 for the branding project. Since then, I've slowly raised my hourly rate as I've grown in experience and skill. While I might be able to work more efficiently and with greater talent now (which lessens the hours it takes to complete the project), my hourly rate has grown as has my expertise (which equals a bigger price for my clients who are happy to pay for high quality). However, at the end of the day, the value of your work is still being confined to the hours you work on a project.

Income/Needs-Based

This approach forces you to first think about how much money you need to live, rather than how much you believe your work is worth. There are a few steps to this process that I've outlined below.

Make A List Of All Your Monthly Expenses

Combine both your business and personal expenses so that you can see what you need to make each month. Of course, you'll want to actually make a profit, so you'll need to add on to that number to do well financially.

Write Down Your Services/Packages

Take a realistic look at how much work you can take on each month, making sure not to overbook yourself. Remember to think about how long a project takes as well as how many individual projects you want to juggle at once.

Price Your Services

This step will look different for everyone but now you get to price your services so that you make your income goal. At this point, you could price per service if applicable, or assign yourself an hourly rate or project rate based on steps number 1 and 2.

This is the most straightforward way to meet a financial goal but it can be hard to plan ahead, especially if your monthly expenses change every month, or you have peak seasons of income and other months that are slow. You should have the average of what you pay every month figured out to know what you need to make.

Another thing that fluctuates from person to person is how much you need to live. Depending on where you live and what type of lifestyle you're used to, your monthly expenses will vary greatly. Sometimes it feels a little weird asking for money that you don't technically need (once you've received enough income to cover expenses), so this approach can feel a little unnatural to some.

Value-Based Rate

With a value-based rate, you base your prices not on the hours you spend but on the value that you're creating for your client's business (think: end result and the benefits your client will receive from working with you). This usually means that you will create a custom quote for each potential client (although it's good to have a bare minimum price that you'll never below).

- To create a value-based price, ask yourself (and the client) these questions:
- How much money is the client already bringing in?
- Are they a big business bringing in over $100k or are they a smaller business or start-up?
- How is their income going to affect their budget? What percent of their budget are they open to using on your service/product?
- What are their business goals and what impact will your services have on accomplishing them? (In other words, what are they expecting from you?)

Example: Your client is launching a new product and you're designing the packaging. The client is planning a $100k launch, so it's vital that the packaging looks high quality and draws in the right customers. This raises the value of your services because the work you do will be playing a huge role in whether they meet their goals or not.

Taxes and Protecting Yourself

There are many different options available for insurance if you are self-employed and/or own your own business. I recommend looking into these seven main groups and finding what works for you based on your needs and business structure. The seven insurance areas we'll look at include health, liability, auto, umbrella, home, life, and long-term disability. You might need to take this chapter in chunks. It's a lot of info and math.

Yeah, if you are lucky you can get any of these from a significant other's job. Though there are now options that can be a lot better than from an employer. Even if you do have one of your hustles, be it a part-time job, I want you to know all the available options. Now that more and more people are not going the traditional route, there are a lot more options out there.

Believe me, I know this isn't any fun. Cause you ain't gonna get away from paperwork. As the saying goes, "nothing is certain except death and taxes".

HEALTH INSURANCE

Monthly health insurance coverage pays for medical expenses (and sometimes dental and optical, depending on the company) by directly paying your medical costs. You can purchase health insurance through multiple venues, depending on your needs.

Your Spouse Has Insurance Through Work

In many situations, a spouse's employer will offer health insurance that both individuals can be on, which is usually cost-effective and convenient. The benefits vary, depending on the company and policy, but it's an option worth exploring if it's available to you.

State Insurance

Every state offers health insurance through the government, usually at reduced rates. You can easily find your state's coverage by visiting healthcare.gov and selecting the state you live in. Coverage varies by state and most programs have a list of accepted clinics and doctors.

Insurance Through Professional Associations

Contact the small business association in your city to find out if they have an insurance program for those who are self-employed. The Small Business Service Bureau, Inc. is a great resource for finding health insurance for you and your family as well as for any employees you may hire.

Health Savings Account

Many people have a health savings account (HSA) that is a savings account you open and add money to that can only be used for medical expenses. Any expense you pay is completely tax-deductible. With an HSA, you'll end up paying more upfront for your healthcare expenses, but you'll pay a lower monthly premium which can be cost-effective.

LIABILITY

Liability insurance is a good idea for small business owners, as it protects you from various issues that may arise with customers and employees. Liability covers a wide range of coverages including third-party bodily injuries and medical payments for employees.

GENERAL LIABILITY INSURANCE

General Liability (GL) protects you in case someone takes legal action against you. GL is customized for your business, so coverage prices vary. Protection includes property damage, physical injury, defense costs as well as personal and advertising injury.

PROFESSIONAL LIABILITY INSURANCE

Professional Liability Insurance (PLI), also called Professional Indemnity Insurance (PII) or more commonly Errors and Omissions (E&O), protects you from having to pay the full cost of defending your business in court and paying damages awarded in a lawsuit. Coverage does not include criminal prosecution. In some areas, PLI is required by law for certain professionals.

BUSINESS OWNER'S POLICY

Business Owner's Policy (BOP) coverage combines general liability insurance and property insurance into a single policy at a reduced rate. It's a flexible option if you need multiple types of coverage.

WORKERS' COMPENSATION

Finally, if you have any employees, this type of coverage is mandatory by law. Workers' Comp will cover employees' lost wages if they're injured at work as well as their medical expenses.

AUTO INSURANCE

There are three types of auto insurance offered at various rates depending on your age, driving record as well as the make and model of your vehicle.

If you're responsible for an accident, liability coverage will cover the costs of injuries or property damage caused by the incident.

Collision

Collision coverage will cover the cost to fix or replace your vehicle if it's damaged or totaled in an accident.

In case of theft, vandalism, flood, fire, or hail, comprehensive coverage will cover any costs or losses.

You also will need extra coverage if you decide to work anything that will require delivery or ride-sharing since you will have to protect yourself and others.

LONG-TERM DISABILITY INSURANCE

In case of an inability to work for a long period of time due to illness or injury, long-term disability insurance protects you from the loss of income. This coverage helps maintain your standard of living until you are able to continue working.

UMBRELLA INSURANCE

An umbrella policy adds an extra layer of protection for your assets that goes beyond your home and/or auto coverage. If your net worth is above $500K, it's a good idea to have an Umbrella Insurance in place.

TERM LIFE INSURANCE

Life Insurance coverage can vary widely, but it's a good idea to have a policy in place in case you pass away and leave behind debt or a family without income.

HOMEOWNERS/RENTERS INSURANCE

In case of an incident (like a fire or tornado), homeowners insurance covers repairing or replacing your house and/or personal belongings. If you rent, renters insurance will replace your belongings in case of a disaster or burglary.

INSURANCE BROKERS

If you're feeling overwhelmed as to how to find the best insurance for your life and business, an insurance broker might be the best way to go. A broker is a professional who will research insurance costs and options for you and recommend the policy that best fits your needs.

TAXES

Sales Tax

Every state has a sales tax, except for Alaska, Delaware, Montana, New Hampshire, and Oregon. If you live in any of the remaining 45 states or Washington D.C., you are responsible for collecting, calculating, and reporting sales tax to both the local and state governments.

Determine if your product or service is subject to sales tax

Retail items like purses and shoes are subject to sales taxes. Prescription medication and food items usually are exempt from sales taxes, though the rules change from state to state. Sales tax gets more complicated if you sell items online or offer digital items. The majority of states now tax digital downloads which include e-books and e-courses. 24 states also require e-commerce sellers to collect and pay sales tax. Usually, medical services and legal services are exempt. Personal services like nail salons, pet grooming, and lawn care are subject to sales tax.

If you are confused about whether your product or service is taxable, it's a good idea to contact your state's tax agency or department of revenue.

Register for sales tax permit

Before you can collect sales tax, you must register for a sales tax permit on your state's department of revenue website. If you do business in more than one state, you'll need to register in each of those states. After registering, you'll receive a sales tax ID that you will use when reporting your sales tax.

Determine the sales tax rate

The sales tax rate that you must charge depends on where you sell. If you sell in multiple states, you'll need to calculate and collect the tax in each of those states.

Charge sales tax for each purchase

To make sales tax calculation easier, try point of sale software that calculates the correct state and local sales tax rates. Make sure your invoice or receipts shows the sales tax on a separate line.

Submit sales tax return

The last step is to submit your sales tax return to the state, along with the payments you've collected from customers. If you use accounting software, you can set it up to have sales tax payments automatically sent to a separate account. Due dates for filing sales tax vary by state. So make sure you know yours.

INCOME & SELF-EMPLOYMENT TAXES

Sole proprietors, LLCs, partnerships, and S-corporations are pass-through entities, which means the business profits are passed through to the owner (that's you!). You are then taxed on your business' profits as an individual and don't have to pay taxes at the corporate level.

Profit does not equal your gross receipts (which is all the income your business receives in a tax year) but is your income (or revenue) minus your expenses. For tax purposes, you're taxed on your revenue minus your tax deductions. (Note: Expenses and tax deductions are similar but not always the same. For example, entertainment costs are a business expense for bookkeeping, but they are not deductible for tax purposes.)

As the government cannot charge you tax from regular payroll income, you are required to pay self-employment taxes instead that are a combination of social security and Medicare.

For 2020, the self-employment tax is 15.3%. C-Corporation and S-Corporation owners, working as employees, are not required to pay this self-employment tax.

The self-employment tax is what makes small business taxes feel unbearably expensive. Unlike employees—whose employers cover Social Security and Medicare payroll taxes—self-employed workers are responsible for paying the whole shebang.

However, you only pay self-employment tax on 92.35% of your profit. The other 7.65% is considered the "employer portion" of your payroll taxes. As in, if you were an employee, your business could deduct the 7.65% contributed to your Social Security and Medicare. So you do get to deduct it!

To summarize:

Income subject to self-employment tax: 92.35% of your profit

Income not subject to self-employment tax: 7.65% of your profit

How to calculate self-employment tax

$100,000 (revenue) -- $30,000 (expenses) = $70,000 (profit)

$70,000 x 92.35% = $64,645 earnings subject to self-employment tax

$64,645 x 15.3% = $9,890 self-employment tax

What are "estimated" taxes?

Estimated taxes are quarterly payments that you make toward your final yearly tax bill on all income that is not subject to withholding (self-employment, interest, dividends, rents, and alimony). Since you don't know how much you'll owe until you file your tax return, these payments are—you guessed it—estimates!

The idea behind estimated taxes is that you pay a portion of what you think your final tax bill will be throughout the year. Then, when you file your taxes, your quarterly payments are applied to your total tax bill, and you pay the difference (or get a refund if you ended up over-paying). If you don't pay your estimated taxes throughout the year, you may be charged a penalty fee when you file your taxes.

Paying your estimated taxes is like paying off a big purchase in installments. Instead of having to muster up the cash to pay a huge tax bill, you pay small bits over time. That way, come tax time, you're not scrambling to pay your taxes or going into tax debt with the IRS. There are handy estimated tax calculators online that can help simplify the process.

Save for your taxes monthly

While you only pay your estimated taxes four times a year, it's best practice to create a monthly tax-saving habit. Saving monthly for taxes ensures you have the cash available to make your payments—and it's better for your cash flow. Putting away $1,000 a month is a lot more doable than paying $3,000 out of the blue!

To save for your taxes monthly, you need to know two numbers:

- Your monthly profit and
- The percentage of it you will save for taxes—A.K.A your tax savings percentage

There's no one-size-fits-all tax savings percentage. Everyone's tax situation is unique, and factors like your income, filing status, dependents, and personal deductions impact your tax savings percentage.

If you have a tax preparer that helps you file your taxes, use their expertise to figure out your tax savings percentage. If you don't have a tax preparer, a good rule of thumb is to start by saving 30% of your monthly profit.

Calculating monthly tax savings

$10,000 monthly revenue − $3,000 monthly expenses = $7,000 monthly profit

$7,000 x 30% = $2,100 in tax savings

(Note: "Tax savings" here means how much you're saving to put toward your tax payments, not how much you avoided paying in taxes.)

Legal

There are some other things you need to keep in mind when getting set up, or even a little way down the line. This is the other side of protecting yourself. Not just from accidents or 'what ifs'. There are some things you need to do with the government to protect yourself. Sadly, if you don't do some of them right, you can also get smacked from them.

Luckily, most of them are pretty easy to do. Just more paperwork and time. A lot of them are even free since you can do most online. The problem is when you don't know what you don't know.

It can seem overwhelming to keep track of the legal details that come with having your own business. Confused what forms are necessary or what you have to report to the state? Read below for an overview on LLCs, trademarks and more.

BANKING

For tax purposes, it's much simpler to have a separate account for business income and expenses. You'll be able to track income and expenses without wading through personal bills and costs. A separate business account will also provide you with protection if you have to provide documentation to the IRS or other services. You'll need an Employer Identification Number to open the account (more on that later).

You should have a checking and a savings account. I use my savings to put my taxes in for my quarterly taxes. I have two separate checking accounts. One for my main business (that several of my hustles live under) and the other is for my freelancing.

DECIDE WHAT KIND OF ENTITY YOUR BUSINESS WILL BE

Now as you start out, you may just start with what is easiest. As a Sole Proprietor, you don't need to do anything upfront. Just need to state it on your taxes. And you will need to talk with an expert to figure out, with how much you make, what entity you should be. But it's perfectly fine to stay as a Sole Proprietor. Even when you have several hustles.

Another thing to think about too is if some of your hustles can fall under an umbrella of like or similar things. Then you could put several of them together

There are three main types of corporations for you to consider for your business:

Limited Liability Corporation

The Limited Liability Corporation (LLC) is a "pass-through" entity where income is reported on individual income tax returns. This provides you with legal protection against lawsuits, without creating an organizational structure that is overly cumbersome.

This is what I have. Mostly because I knew that I wanted to grow it to something bigger than what I had in the beginning. Plus I wanted some added protection, but I didn't want or need the added bulk of a bigger corporation.

C-Corporation

A C-Corporation legally separates owners' assets and income from that of the business. This limits the liability of investors and owners since you can only lose the amount of money that has been invested. A C-Corporation is required to hold annual meetings and have a board of directors. You'll pay tax on the business' income, plus tax on whatever income you receive as an owner or employee.

S-Corporation

The main difference between a C-Corp and an S-Corporation is taxes. S-Corporations don't pay tax; instead, you (and other owners) report the business income as personal revenue. This can be lucrative in building up an unencumbered startup. This way, more of the invested money will go towards growing the business instead of paying taxes.

STATE REGISTRATION

To legally register your business, you'll need to complete

forms from your state-specific Secretary of State website. The paperwork varies per state, as does the cost of filing. You will have to regularly re-register as well, so make sure to note the timeframe your state requires.

I was lucky that I found someone who could do my taxes that also could renew all my state stuff for my business. But you should have all this stuff and everything else in a secure place. Plus have everything scheduled out to remind you to update everything.

STATE TAX ID NUMBER

Check to see if your state requires you to obtain a State Tax ID Number, which you'll use when filing taxes. Again, this might vary based on your location. Thankfully, this application was all online and fairly simple to complete. For example, the website I used was www.tap.state.nm.us. It took a few days for my application to be approved and I received my number via email.

DOING BUSINESS AS

Doing Business As (DBA) – This step is only required if you're going to be operating under a name other than your legal name. For example, someone's legal name is Sarah Elizabeth Black but her business name is Sarah Elizabeth. I would not need to file a DBA since the names are the same.

Now, since I call my business Courageous Creativity, I needed to file a DBA since my business name differs from my legal name. Easy, right?

If you need to apply for a DBA, your state and/or local county will be able to provide you with the paperwork. Give them a quick call or email and they can point you in the right direction. That's what they're there for!

IRS REGISTRATION

Think you'll have to register your business with the IRS? Nope! Surprised? I was.

The only thing that you'll have to do with the IRS in regards to your business is complete the Schedule C Profit or Loss from Business Form (1040), along with your personal tax return if you're registered as a Sole Proprietor or single-member LLC.

Honestly, unless you are trained in this, get professional help. They will know what you will need to do and not get in trouble. You don't want to mess this up, the Government wants their cut of the money.

EMPLOYER IDENTIFICATION NUMBER

We're almost there, I promise! Here is where you'll acquire an Employer Identification Number, also known as EIN. While this step is NOT mandatory, it is highly encouraged and required if you're planning on opening a business bank account or hiring employees.

The purpose of an EIN is to use in place of your social security number on tax forms. Did that sell you on wanting to get one? What if I mentioned it's completely free and quite simple to complete? I knew I'd convert you.

You can only obtain an EIN during the week (Mon-Fri, 7 am – 10 pm EST) at IRS.gov. Once you've completed the steps on the website, you obtain the number immediately, and it never expires. Sweet!

BUSINESS TRADEMARK

You have the option to trademark your business. This step is NOT mandatory. Trademarking your businesses is added protection if you want to make a brand with many components to it.

The most common reason to trademark is to help your business stand out. If you want to keep anyone else from creating a similar business name, you'll need to have your business trademarked. This is usually helpful if you have a bigger business or do most of your business online.

While you can acquire the trademark on your own, it's a long and complicated process best done by hiring a lawyer. It will not be cheap, but there are lawyers and groups out there that will help tiny, creative businesses for a smaller price. Spend time researching what class (or classes) you want your trademark to fit into, as well as any sub-classes. Each sub-class adds up in fees, so be specific in exactly what you need.

Not sure what I'm talking about? I still don't completely get it either. I just told my lawyer everything I do and wanted to do and she gave me an overview of what classes would cover them. Now, at least twice a year I have to ask if something is covered in my trademark. Mostly because legal jargon makes my eyes cross.

After a few years I got my trademark for most online things, a lot of apparel, written products, and a few others. Honestly, it would be hard to explain quickly and easily. But I got the ones for what I did within my business.

But you do need to remember to defend your trademark. You have to keep on top of others using it and if they overlap with which trademark classes you have. It is an added cost to have a lawyer to draft a letter. Most of the time once they get the official letter, people change what they are doing.

Believe me, you want a lawyer for this. They will have the knowledge and expertise to know all the pieces. I've had to defend my trademark a few times already. And since they already had the info on my trademark, they were able to check out the offender and draft up an email for me to send. And usually that's all that's needed. Only once have I had to send a second email, that was a lot less nice. But this is my brand and cost a pretty penny, don't fuck with me.

For most side hustles, when you are not doing very big or different things, this is not necessary. But if you want to grow it to something more or it really starts to take off it's an added protection for you. Because there are a lot of people who will try to steal from others just to make a quick buck.

WEBSITE

It's important (and required by federal law) to have these two items on your website:

Terms & Conditions

There are no legal requirements for what you deem "terms and conditions," but it's helpful for your users to understand the rules for using your website, including purchases and returns. Always include a notice of trademark and/or copyright (example: "Copyright©2020, Your website.com") and a statement that limits your liability if there are errors on the website.

Privacy Policy

If you're gathering any personal information from your users, you need a privacy policy in place. The purpose of a Privacy Policy is to inform users of how you will be collecting their data in order to protect their privacy.

Both of these need to be written with legal jargon. So make sure you chose the right one. I will share some of the ones I've used in Appendix II. But with them being written legally, they will all be dated. So you will need to update all of them at the beginning of the year. Plus add in your own name / site name.

The best place to have them is as their own pages on your site. Then have them linked at the footer. That way, they will be available on every page.

WRITE IT ALL DOWN

Everything needs to be in writing! OK, you have a boilerplate contract. Is that enough to count as "everything"?

Probably not! Some examples of what you need to make sure that you have 'put it in writing' include:

- Customer agreements/contracts
- Estimates/Invoices
- Disclaimers
- Terms of Services
- Warranties
- Employment agreements
- Business relationship agreements (e.g., with vendors)

Remember to be detailed in your writings. Always include party names, dates, contact information, details of each party's duties and expectations, and so on where applicable. There are a lot of free templates out there to get you started. But at some point, it would be a good idea to get a lawyer to make custom ones or look over the ones you have and add things that are specific to your business.

You can find a lawyer who works with creatives that can be a lot cheaper than a traditional one who can just give you suggestions on what to add (for a fee of course). Then you can look for templates or examples to pull from. There are also shops where you can buy contracts and such for a price. These are usually much more detailed with a lot more pieces. You can later take parts out that you don't need.

Beyond these official documents, it is best to put what you may consider casual conversations in writing. If a court case ever arises about a customer's expectations about your work and you can prove something by showing an email versus stating you had a conversation about it, you will be well ahead of the game.

Multiple Streams Of Income

Now you may be a little overwhelmed just starting the first one. It's perfectly fine to only have the one and still have a job. It may be the only one you want or need.

Remember, you wanted to do this for a little extra money, to test the waters, or to be more creative. And having the one side hustle gives you that, you do not have to go any farther.

But perhaps you have the itch again. The first one has gotten to the point where you can take less time, money, and effort then run it. Or you do not want to push the hustle to full time but want to make more money (to maybe replace your full-time job). Then you may be ready to start another one.

I know a lot of you are sitting there wide-eyed. Like you can't even fathom starting another one. You think I'm crazy. But you're looking at this the wrong way.

You can get to a point with any hustle where it can mostly run itself, or only need you for short bursts. There are a lot of people or programs out there that can take a lot of your tasks off your hands.

There are times in your life when you have more time and space to work on other things. You squeeze in a vacation when your kids are out of school. Spend a whole weekend doing some DIY in your home.

There is only so much you can say that your time is taken up. How much do you do for your family because you got tired of always asking them? Or doing extra work, outside of office hours because you don't set any boundaries with your boss and coworkers?

I don't mean you need to throw everything out just so you can devote all your free time to your hustles. I seriously want you to do the opposite with your life.

Go back to your list of other possible side hustles. Since you most likely started with one that you had some passion for, look for one that won't take much time or effort to get up and running. Maybe something that will be mostly passive, just needing some maintenance and marketing every once in a while like an e-book or e-course.

A lot of people, even the Small Business Administration, like to flaunt that most small businesses fail within the first five years. What no one tells you is that mostly applies to big capital endeavors. On the low end the maximum number of employees is 250. They can be Sole Proprietorships to privately own Corporations. So it's a range.

It also doesn't go over whether people merge their business with another they have or even change names (which actually happens a lot). It even has the range of how much you make from the maximum from $750,000 - $1.3 million. Though I'd love to have my businesses and side hustles get up into the millions, that's not where most of us are going to be.

But that's not to say that you can't get up there through

multiple hustles. You can get to the upper 6 figures if you know your market, play to your strengths, and deliver a good product/service.

WHY HAVING MULTIPLE STREAMS OF INCOME IS IMPORTANT

We have all seen how easily people can lose their jobs. The thing that society has told us was the safe and secure thing to do. I'm not going to go into the downfalls in our Capitalist society. Essentially that we work in a Capitalist world, but are not Capitalists ourselves since so many of us do not own the big thing in our lives.

It's harder for so many to even afford to buy a place. We are all one big emergency expense away to getting in trouble. One medical problem to being behind on bills, losing a vehicle, or getting kicked out of their place. We definitely do not have a say in the places we work. They need us for the work, but most do not feel any loyalty to us. But we are expected to give it from our end.

The one thing that I figured out that is actually awful is that the largest form of theft in the US is wage theft. Only five states have any laws for protection of it, but most cases don't even go to court. Mostly because prosecutors only want to pursue the big cases. So if your paycheck is short for weeks or even months, it's up to you to sue your employer to get the money. Most companies don't even get fined for doing this yearly. Even in the not-so-depressing-direction, the career you go for may have so much upward mobility. And if you love where you work, but want to save for more or even to prepare for retirement. And you are not looking for something huge. Maybe only an extra thousand a month.

Honestly, having something of your own is what I believe is the real security.

But one of the main things you need to step up is to really be good at having multiple side hustles. And that is a level of organizing that is far higher then what is needed for just one.

The difference between organizing a squad and mobilizing an army. The difference between a socially married couple with demanding jobs, and a family with 3 kids who all have sports and activities with vacations and visiting all the extended family on every holiday. Where everyone has 10 appointments, someone is sick, and only one person can drive.

With any side hustle, there are ebbs and flows and seasons. Times where it is more busy than others. Times where you need to do more marketing, be more visible and advertise, and others where you need to take stock and order things.

The side hustle you first started can be up all year round. But it's the spring and winter holiday times that are really busy for you. So March to ramp up marketing and ordering more inventory, April and May to really sell, and June to wind down and stock. The same applies for March through December.

That's five months that you could do a seasonal hustle. That could only take you 2 months to do. Or another year round one that has the opposite ebbs and flow as the first.

Having more than one can also fuel the other. On the one hand, making enough to afford an endeavor that takes more upfront. Whether that's in inventory or setup.

But there is another way in that it fuels it with more energy. Most of our side hustles will be solo and though what you decide to do may not be creative in itself, it will take creativity.

In how you get the word out, set up your website, or your initial processes. Most of us will not have an expert or mentor to walk us through everything we do. We will need to take the knowledge we have and all the free info we can scrounge up to make things work.

Diverse creative activities can feed each other. But there are so few that are willing to look outside their main field.

That can be one of the main drivers to why so many are unwilling to have more than one side hustle. That they must focus on only one thing. Not creating it into a big business is somehow a failure.

Or that you started your first hustle from your experience from your job. That you may have run out of ideas that interest you from that area. That they cannot see the other options around them.

There has been a constant push, at least since the Industrial Revolution, to always be efficient. It has changed how schools teach, getting us ready for mind-numbing assembly line work.

Now we don't all work in factories anymore, but the same mentality works, especially in the idea of "Master of One" and the 10,000 hours to be a master. That we all must focus on one thing in life and spend all our time in honing that skill.

Don't get me wrong, I want my doctor to have mastery. Same as an architect and really anyone who has to do something close to perfect or people die. But there is so much out there that does not require this amount of energy. The average office worker doesn't need precision. Hell, we've all made mistakes at work and no one died from it (crap, I hope not).

Not all of us are made to master one specific thing. Just as some people do great in a 9 to 5 job and want to just leave it at work, there are people who cannot do the same thing everyday. They want more in what they do in life. Whether its variety, how much they can make, or what time of the day they work. They choose what they want to work on, letting in more creativity and excitement.

I'd like to expand from the mindset chapter. Those are really good steps that I believe everyone needs to work on, no matter what. And it's ongoing work that will take some time to unpack. Since most of them were hammered into you for years.

But really letting yourself live a life farther out of the norm then before. It will be hard to believe that you can live a good life with several side hustles that, by themselves, would make you homeless. That you can do one for only a few months and then let it go.

I have gone through at least thirty different side hustles to where I am now. And I will be adding some more in the future. At the beginning, it was just to explore what I did and did not like.

Some had shit hours, but paid decently and I actually had fun. Others paid OK and had decent hours, but I was bored out of my mind. I've learned throughout the years that I can handle crap hours for things that were not a regular basis and as long as it was fun.

My three main worlds for my business are freedom, creativity, and fun. Those are the most important things to me for everything in my life.

ADDING ON OR SOMETHING NEW

When deciding to add more hustles there always the consideration on whether to keep to the theme or go a completely different direction. Of course you should start the next one when the first is making 'enough' and is stable. Then adding more when the one before is ready too.

If you have a dog food delivery service you also add some of your own merchandise. You can add a dog walking service or sell baked treats. They do not have to connected to delivery part. You can have a completely different brand to the next part. Or keep them together.

You may just want to try something different also. A different area, time commitment, energy, or whether or not you stay home for it. I love creating fun apparel, its passive, but I also do freelance work. For just a few hours a day I've done social media ad rating. Just having something that I know is constant and kind of mindless.

DUMP THE EXCESS

Of course going this route can be anxiety-inducing. The only way to really have multiple side hustles is to get rid of other things in your life. Just like everything else, there's only so much time and energy. And for most, you need to get rid of your job because the point is to replace its income with the things you want to build.

Now that can be hard for many because to them, a job is a known security. And going off and doing all this on your own, while definitely freeing, doesn't have a known track record.

There is a thing where people, having so much time on their hands, don't know how to manage it. They are so used to having a set time to work and mostly be told what to do. That the hustle, the first start, which was thriving, starts to go down.

Part of this can be because you didn't figure out how to work your time for the better. You don't have set times for taking calls or meetings. You check your email whenever you think about it. But there are two other reasons that most don't know. The first is that you have much empty time that doesn't create a drive for you to get your work done quicker. When you had a job, you had to fit in your side hustle in between that and other obligations.

With multiple hustles you need to have set time and days you will work on things. All my backend stuff; social media, emails, inventory, scheduling, etc is done on Mondays. I only do podcast interviews Tuesdays - Thursdays. I write a list for what I need to do each week and divide them up to my days, but also have a side list of things that are coming up or side things I want to do. So if I have time I can still fill my working time with productive things. But I also set my times for my breaks.

Setting Up Systems

There is enough research out there that no one does multi-tasking well. But when running several side hustles, on top of hobbies, friends and family, it is possible to do several things within a day.

Of course you need to know yourself and know what you can handle. Since a side hustle is small and lean, with a little adjusting, you can fit it into your life. But once you start adding multiple ones, other things will need to give in.

You need to have a handle on your time and schedule. You need to know how long things actually take for you to do. Whether it's all your kids' activities, volunteering at an animal shelter, or getting together with your in-laws.

WHAT DO YOU ACTUALLY DO WITH YOUR TIME?

The first thing I tell people when they are really getting into their side hustle is to schedule out their time. That is the first system they need to establish. Schedule out everything in their day. See where there is space for anything. Or figure out what things can be taken out or done differently.

By this time, you have already run one successful side hustle. So you know what goes into it. Everything I'll be giving to you here will first be done to your first side hustle.

To cut down on the time, you need to work in it and make it more efficient. Then you can work on the next one(s).

There will always be a learning curve for each one that you do. Even if any of them are close to the first one you create. Then when you get that one to be profitable (or as you are building it), start implementing these again.

KNOWING WHAT ALL IS NEEDED

Not gonna lie, this part will not be fun. It will take a while and it's tedious. But you will be so grateful to have it done. And that's to list everything you have to do in your hustle with actual instructions on how to do them.

This is an SOP (Standard Operating Procedure) and every business / hustle needs one. Can't really know where you can improve until you can see everything.

And I mean to write down everything. Every. Single. Thing. Every little step you do in your hustle. Don't worry about being too organized. Just keep your steps for each task together.

After you get everything out, then you can organize it all. But it's up to you how you do it. Put it in order of when they need to be down, how you batch them together, or by different categories. Whatever makes sense to you and can be explained to others.

SCHEDULING

As I've said before, you need to figure out what kind of time you have around your work and family. You need to at least have an idea how much time you need and generally what days you do them. Acuity and Calendly are the main programs that most use to schedule.

TIME BLOCKING

There is research that we can only concentrate for a certain amount of time. It's pretty straight-forward. You take certain blocks of time to only work on certain things. Whether it's one type of thing or one specific task.

It can be hard to tackle your to-do task when there are so many things you need to do, and some that are neverending. So you can get lost in checking your emails all day or even just doing your business social media. It's an easy rabbit hole to fall into.

The key to this is organizing the tasks that need to be completed and then set aside a specific timeframe to focus only on those items. This prevents multitasking and interruptions.

This makes you stop and figure out how much time tasks actually take to get accomplished. No mindlessly going back over things just to feel like you're doing something.

You will be more productive and will get tasks done quicker. Plus, the smaller tasks will more likely get done since you will not be going back and forth over and over again. Instead of switching gears, you dedicate 100% on that one task.

This is also as good a place to stack like tasks together.

STACKING

Once you get into the rhythm of things, you start to figure out what things can be done together. Or what order works best. In the same vein of habit stacking, like you take a shower to brush your teeth to flossing. These things always go together.

It makes it less likely you will procrastinate these parts because they all go together in your head. I always brush my teeth after I shower, it doesn't even take a thought to do. You can also have a better idea how long things can take you when they are all together, instead of getting overwhelmed with 20 small things you need to do. Being together you know they only take 30 minutes to do together because they all need to be done on the computer.

When I did my blog on my own, I did all my graphics at the same time and all my social media as well. Mostly because I didn't want to have to come back and remember all the information. It was already at the top of my mind and it was easier to summarize, With some of it being somewhat repeated.

MANAGEMENT SYSTEMS

Now I'm all for getting someone or something to take the load off for me. And there are a lot of great management systems out there to do specific things to most of the things you need done on the back-end.

Now not every side hustle will need a management system. They are good if you have actual clients you have to work with, a team who does different parts, and have several projects going on at the same time. These are photographers, wedding planners, coaches, and consultants, just to name a few.

They help with all the emails you need to send, questionnaires, contracts, invoices, and even be on top of payment plans. They can send you and the client reminders on everything and keep all the information in one central place.

These are more for businesses with services than products, especially if you have specific projects or many different things your clients need.

Dubsado, Honey book, 17Hats are about the same thing. They are a system, mostly in the wedding industry but others can adapt to it, to help keep you and your clients on top of all the tasks that need to be done. Business management all in one. Each a little different on how they work so you'll need to try them out to see what one you like better.

ORGANIZING

When you get several hustles going, family, hobbies, and possibly a full time job, it can be a little overwhelming with all the little details. Getting something up that houses all your steps, projects, and just to-do lists in one place will keep you from pulling out your hair.

Asana is usually used for teams or if you have a bigger project you need to work on, especially if you and another person need to go back and forth to keep it moving. The most recent project I did was with a graphic designer to redo my website. She needed me to give all the info of what I needed done, the copy, any images, and my logos. She kept me up to date on each part that was done so I could ask for changes as we went along.

Trello is more yourself or your team. It's mostly just a fancy list maker. It lets you create boards for any project or task. You can put in all the info that needs to do the task. You can check things off and rearrange. It's a good place to have all your SOPs so anyone can reference it for any task.

ACCOUNTING

Handling your money is very important. And with having several hustles (or even a business thrown in) you need to keep on top of what money is combing in and all your expenses. There are several really good programs that can help.

However, most of them will not be able to do all that you need to do. But any little bit helps. At some point, you may just want to hire someone to do this for you.

Spreadsheets

Can't really talk about accounting without at least touching on the easiest thing to start with as a good old spreadsheet. Your side hustle may not be very complicated with what you do and expenses so having just this may be all you need.

It's not hard to look online to figure out extra fancy things you can add to them. Add in calculations to add together different rows for you. Or add in tax for a product you do. There's even places that will give you their spreadsheets they've created for their own. And the best thing is you can change for what you need at any time.

Wave

This is a basic accounting system that is online. It can connect most of your bank accounts and organize what goes in and out. Over the years, they have added a few more things, but again it's more for less needs.

QuickBooks

Not gonna lie, this is the granddaddy of them all. QuickBooks can be used for your personal finances, freelancing, and a full business. If you're just doing a few simple side hustles, you can just do the freelance version. But now that I have a full business and a little too many to count hustles, I need to use the full version.

This is not free but definitely worth the price. The best part is that you can write off the cost on your taxes.

SOCIAL MEDIA

When it comes to marketing on social media platforms, you should be on several. Luckily, there is a lot out there that can schedule a lot of what you post. And most of them are free up to a point. But the best part it's just how many times you can post a month than just only for a short time.

There are some that only give you so many before you have to pay. These are usually for ones that are more narrow in what they do, specifically working for only one social media platform. But being able to schedule will let you batch this work ahead of time. Plus you get analytics to see what is working or not and they give you insights to what you are doing.

Scheduling can alleviate the anxiety of what to post in the moment. You can organize them better seeing that you talk about your services on Tuesdays and Thursdays, then behind-the-scenes of Friday. You can figure out marketing ahead of time for special dates and holidays.

The first ones I'll talk about are ones that will cover more than one platform, Buffer and Meet Edgar. They are both basically the same. They are made to post to multiple sites – Twitter, Facebook, Pinterest, Instagram, and a few others depending on the scenario. Buffer is free for certain social media and for a certain amount of posts scheduled per week. It's an easier way to keep a presence in more places.

Planoly and Later are the big names with regard to posting to Instagram. There used to be more but many of them lost their permission to do so. The best part of these two is that they are free to post to your feed for 30 posts a month. For most, that is plenty. Planoly has started to allow posting to Pinterest as well. It seems to be a good fit since both are image-heavy. They do not let you schedule stories or IGTV right now.

Tailwind is the main scheduler for Pinterest. It has the most integration. It is only free for the first 30 posts scheduled. They also rolled out posting to Instagram. The difference is that if you have one post that can go into multiple boards, you can schedule them out in intervals. And even campaigns that you can add any number of posts that go out over a period of time.

EMAIL

What having a website is to being on sites like Etsy, having your own email list is to social media. Social media is rented space. You own your email list. And it is a direct connection to people who follow you.

We are all tired of getting so many emails. Some people can get hundreds in a day (y'all need to start unsubscribing or putting those things into spam) and most of it is junk. But you need to have a list. A direct connection to your fans and clients. You want to give them updates, new products, or even sales. Of course, don't be spammy when sending to your people. Have a general schedule when you send out whether its weekly up to monthly.

You will need your own email address to connect to these. But they will forward anything that gets sent to your email from whatever you sent out. There are several that are free up to a certain number of subscribers or emails sent. Each one has a different amount of customization. Of course the ones that cost give you more.

It depends on your needs. I always start off with something free. You won't have a big list for a while. Customizing with logos, different colors, and dividing those on the list into different categories may not be necessary.

MailChimp, Mailerlite, and Convertkit have free options. You can send out as much as long as you have under 1,000 subscribers. They are great places to start with. The first two are very basic in their design, with Convertkit at a little more. It depends on what you want and think you can handle.

CALENDARS AND SCHEDULING

Having all your calls and appointments organized is really important, whether you have client work, appointments for proposals, or just know what times you have to do work. While I love a paper planner for the year and week, I still need an electronic calendar to keep on top of everything.

You already need to know how much time you have free for a side hustle, but you need to schedule working on it. Or other things will take over that time. Whether it's family or just that dreaded to-do list.

I have two podcasts right now that have some interviews. So some weeks I can have recordings with 3–4 people so I need to know what times are available to schedule them, plus how to work everything else around them. You really need a place that has all your things that cover all your outside obligations.

Google Calendars

Not gonna lie, I'm a fan of Google products. Like almost everything, they have this free. Plus I can use it over my phone, iPad, laptop, and desktop. And they give reminders over everything that has the app and to your email that's connected. Of course, there are other free versions out there that will connect over many different devices.

Calendly and Acuity

Something you need for others to make appointments with you. Set up a coaching call, podcast interview, or to just set up your services. We've all been on those messages where you go back and forth with the person on what days you're available in the morning. But they only have afternoons then. How about Thursday? No, I have to get the kids. Then you're moving on to the next week.

These two programs take that out of your hands. You set up what days and times you are available. Maybe you only take calls for client work Tuesdays, Wednesdays, and Thursdays. It connects to your calendar (multiple for a price); so anything you put on there doesn't get overlapped. Create buffer time around them. You can even set it up that you only allow two of those kinds of calls a day.

This way, you just have to send the link to your scheduler and they can find a time that works for them. It automatically gets it on your calendar and they will send out a reminder to you and the other person. Easy peasy!

Now, having so much up electronically can be great. Being able to get to your stuff over different computers, tablets, and phones streamlines everything. But the thing is, some things just don't work for people online. Some of us just like to do things old school with pen and paper.

DO WHAT WORKS FOR YOU

Don't get me wrong, I do a lot of my stuff online. The convenience is worth it. But not everyone can as organized online, its just a preference.But I am a pen and paper kind of gal. I can't even tell you how many pens, notebooks, and journals I have... Let's just say there are some big ass bins tucked away.

I have at least half of all my organization not done electronically. All my brainstorming and planning is done in a notebook. Then every side hustle or project gets its own notebook. I have several whiteboard calendars up around the house so I can glance at the big things I have on my schedule. Then even a weekly desk calendar for all of my specific tasks for each day. Different worksheets I created to track all my bills, personal and professional as well as my saving goals and podcast episodes. Each episode shows when it gets published and the five main tasks, they all have boxes to check them off.

I know I'm missing a few other things I do that's physical, but these are literally the ones that are around my desk right now. This is my style and it works for me. For others, it may sound very chaotic.

And that's perfectly fine. We each have our own style and preferences. You're gonna have to figure out which parts work for you. That's why I made sure to give as many free options up above, or at least decent free trials. And the best part is that for a lot of them, you may not have the need to upgrade.

I hate when there used to only be options that only worked when you were really small and didn't want any personalization. They were made for you to not use them in the long term. And then you had to upgrade to something – a list more complicated and really expensive. That was especially true for email marketing.

How To Hire Help

The best part (for me) when it comes to side hustles is that you can do it all yourself. But more in that you don't need expensive schooling or training. Most things you want to try have a cheap version to get you started.

But there comes a point where something has to give. We all try to have too much on our plate. Playing with the kids. Hanging out with friends. Or with me just adding one more hustle. I swear it's only for a few months, just to try it out...

So it's time to ask for help. Now you may be lucky enough to have some people who can help you with the kids or who have a place for you to go for a few hours to work on things. But if you want good help that's timely, you're gonna have to pay for it.

There is nothing wrong with that. As we went over in the Mindset chapter, you can't do everything yourself. But I have to elaborate on this more. Not just to get help with one of the things to save you time or to automate things in a program; you want to start looking for help all the time.

Now this can be in your personal life or within your side hustles. Wherever you think will be the most helpful and relieve the most pressure. Hell, just to take things off your hands you just don't like to do. Anyone else hate dusting as much as I do?

Had a couple of friends who wanted to do a YouTube channel about DIY but with a funny twist. They wanted to make it useful in showing people how to do things, but also wanted to show how things could go wrong. Some ways to fix that or how to avoid them. Even having parts where they mess things up or are getting so confused they just pay someone to do it in the end.

They wanted to call it "Rob Writes A Check" and I thought it was brilliant since the guy named 'Rob' was not handy at all. The other guy was decently handy, but in the redneck-this-should-work way. And I have seen them try to work on things around the house. It was funny, but I'd probably would have gotten pissed if I had to live with them.

'Cause half the time they couldn't do what needed to be done or it was just 'good enough' so Rob just 'wrote a check' and paid for someone to do it right and not have to look at the janky thing that would of "worked" but did not look good or didn't work all the time.

And that's where you will get eventually. Doing every part of your hustle, but not everything is great or up to the standard you want or need. We can't be great at everything we do. And you need to come to a point where you decide to get someone who is great at the stuff you aren't (or really don't want to do anymore) to do it for you.

FYI, they never made the channel. So if anyone wants to take the idea, I won't be mad.

FIGURING OUT YOUR PAIN POINTS

Once you start having a good paying hustle, you will more than likely know one thing that you don't want to do anymore. It may take you too long, the results aren't great, or you're just done doing it. Which is great, that's you keeping an eye out to what can be upgraded.

And that's how you should look at getting help, not as a failure, but as upgrading your life. Isn't that the point of the hustles?

Now, before you start looking for people you need to do some math. Some of you may be a little upset since we did a bunch of chapters before. But this will be simple. Take the average of what you make in a month from your hustle(s), then subtract the costs of running it and the cost of paying yourself. Now paying yourself you can have set up to be a paycheck every two weeks. Just a percentage of what you make. Or this could be just the amount you want saved for that vacation or what you put in every month. Of course the cost of running should include the taxes and whatever is left over is what you can use to run things better.

The reason why I only say the money from your hustles is because if you have a regular job, I don't want you to rely on that too much. That should be for all your bills and personal stuff. You wouldn't have the hustle if you could afford everything you wanted already. The money is part of it or you would just do it as a hobby.

You already have your list of tasks you do. (You better have one for setting up your systems.) It may not be up to you what gets taken off your list first. There are some things you will not be able to do on a small budget.

You can go two ways with this, but the main point is that whatever you get help with needs to release more time for you to make more money. It's either the things that you have doing or that take up the most time. If you're lucky, you have something that falls into both categories. It'll be up to you as to what would be the most beneficial. If you have a task that would literally save you hours a week to have someone else to do, then that's your choice. And you need to remember that just because it takes you a long time to do it, doesn't mean it would for someone with more experience. It may only cost you a couple of hundred bucks a month to have someone else to do it.

Now if you have a task that you actually, seriously loathe then that might be your choice. You dread doing it every time and expend a lot of energy hating doing it. It may only give you a little time back, but also saves the emotion, energy, and motivation drainage.

WHERE TO FIND HELP ONLINE

Sometimes all the help we need is at the back-end of stuff. Even for me who grew up with the Internet there are some things I'm just not good with. I can set up and do basic coding for my website but I'm a little hopeless with my copy. Yes, I know that's a little ironic being a writer....

Facebook

Honestly the most wide variety of and quality of people I've found have been in Facebook groups. Finding some decent groups isn't too hard once you know what to look for.

And once you are in a couple, you can see where else others are in too to join. A lot of these groups will have a day that you can post on a thread that you are looking for someone to do something or someone to put up what they do.

There is less pressure to pick someone there. You can just ask for people's links or portfolio to see if they are what you need, in your price range, or even vibe with you.

Most of the people who work online and not in person will be more than likely to be in contract. So make sure you get them a 1099 for tax purposes. You can find anyone to really do anything.

But it can be hard to find one person for many different jobs/projects you can have since so many people have their own niches. However, some will branch out some to fill a need.

I found the best photographers and graphic designers on Facebook. Hell, some of them are even doing their work as side hustles as well.

Referrals

We all trust the people in our lives (well, most of them for some stuff) and when they say they love or hate someone or something, we listen. Just as when we want referrals from past customers, we do the same thing when looking for a product or service.

Once you start building a network, whether it's people in the business and those around you, you start to notice some of the similarities that you need help getting done.

NEED TO BE IN PERSON

Sometimes we will build a hustle that will need to be in person, so getting help too will be necessary. These can be one-off projects that you need from time to time or people on a regular basis.

You may have started your lawn care hustle on your own, but you got the interest to grow it. But you can only do so many in a day. That's when you hire some helpers to take on some of those clients. Or to help you with bigger projects. Someone to help speed things up for you.

Or you may want someone who will help you set up your tables at a farmer's market or pop-up shop. Maybe even take some shifts to man it for you so you don't have to be there from the beginning to end every single day.

The point, again, is that someone else will be taking something off your hands. Either so you can work more on the stuff that only you can do, A.K.A the money-making, or so you can enjoy your time off. Like what you planned with starting your hustles.

Indeed

If you're looking for a larger pool of possible candidates,

this is a good place to look. It's actually not hard to post a job there. Not gonna go over it with you, they have good instructions on the site.

It's nice for finding people who don't fit into the Facebook groups that you decide to go into. A lot of the ones I'm in are very creative. Though I do usually need someone who is creative since that's a lot of what I do, not everybody thinks they fall into that description.

You also need to be very descriptive in your job post, have good keywords and tags, and actually have a budget up front. Plus, you are not having to interact with each person that wants the job. On Facebook you can be fielding DMs for weeks from aggressive people. There is a lot more separation on Indeed.

There is also some added security on both ends, though you still need to do your due diligence in vetting people and possibly checking them. I don't know, I just have seen more people out there to be more serious about the job.

Now, most of what I've talked about is making things easy within your hustle. But there are other things you can do just to make life easier and that is to hire for things in your everyday life. And I already touched on the idea that some have that these kinds of things are "supposed" to be your responsibility. Everyone gets the pressure, but moms get it more. That they are somehow supposed to do everything for their family and they are failures if they don't. And do it all effortlessly.

Where the hell is it that that's a rule for being an adult?

For those who grew up poor, you needed to do everything yourself. Anything goes wrong with your car or the toilet, you try to fix it on your own. Because calling a service is an expense you can't afford. And you just fix it enough for it to work, hopefully for a while.

But the point of making more money is to afford time to do the things you want. Which means taking things away that you do not want to do. Parents get a babysitter so they can go on a date. I could care less what the hell goes on with my car. I'll take care of it, but I get no joy in cleaning it or getting any of the normal maintenance done. Yeah, it can be cheaper to change the oil myself, but that's a couple hours I just don't want to do.

Who says you can't have a cleaner come by twice a month to do the deep cleaning in your house? You're not lazy to hire someone to pick up all your leaves in Fall. Hell, it's smart to get someone else to pick up all the dog poop in your yard. There's already services that will do your grocery shopping for you. Drop your dog off for daycare every once in a while so you don't have to walk them every day after work.

So go through all the things you have to do and pick some that you would love to never have to do again. Check to see what extra money you have and get someone else to do at least one of those things. I would rather not do dishes anymore while my friend literally gets anxiety with all the laundry she has to do. Dishes are relaxing for her while I just have clothes for myself working from home and no kids. Each needs are different.

Don't automatically assume that what you want will be expensive. There are a lot of businesses and hustles out there giving a wide range of prices. Maybe you don't get the full cleaning service but have someone come in once a month to scrub your bathroom. Nothing says you can't hire your cousin to go through your emails and unsubscribe from all the crap you don't want.

The point is to free up your time and get money to make life easier.

Conclusion

The possibilities are endless out there. And I hope I've shown you, even in tough times, that there are options to getting yourself out of living paycheck-to-paycheck. You just gotta be brave enough to try.

Especially since I've shown that it's not life or death to try things out, to stop doing any of them, and to fail. Each part is a lesson; so don't let each change of direction discourage you. That is a part of life. It would be boring if you did the exact same thing every day, every week, every year.

Find those sweet spots that give you good money, you can enjoy, and expand your freedom. This will not be an easy road. There will be a lot of ups and down, worrying on failing, figuring out that something is awful, but also finding out that things are absolutely fun. But the uncertainty is part of the fun. This road is not for everyone.

Some people will be happy with just one hustle to save for one thing some of the time. And for them, security is more important. Which is perfectly fine, the world needs people like that. They are just as important.

But some people are just like me, not satisfied with a prescribed life. Wanting something 'other', that's its own shape. Something that changes over and over. And wanting that does not make us weird or destined to fail.

You get to choose how you life goes. In this world we

need to make money to survive so there's no reason to be miserable doing it. Since its going to take up most of your days.

Of course I hope more people will have several side hustles. Because money gives you freedom and independence. So if your job makes some changed that don't involve you, you will not be in trouble with a buffer. You can take the time to find new, maybe better, work. Or you can just not go back to a job. You get to decide. I'm for sure going to keep starting more side hustles and making my money. There's so much out there. You just need to believe it.

And I hope you choose your own freedom.

APPENDIX I

BOOKS

Get Rich, Lucky Bitch: *Release Your Money Blocks and Live a First-class Life*
  By Denise Duffield-Thomas, 2013

Chillpreneur: *The New Rules for Creating Success, Freedom, and Abundance on Your Terms* By Denise Duffield-Thomas, 2019

Making a Living Without a Job: *Winning Ways for Creating Work That You Love* By Barbara J. Winter, 2009

The 4-Hour Workweek: *Escape 9-5, Live Anywhere, and Join the New Rich* By Timothy Ferris, 2009

The No-nonsense Guide to Avoiding Scams and Generating Real Income From Anywhere! By Caitlin Pyle

Imagination Transforms Everything: *Rewrite your Life's Story With "intentional Imagining"* by Andrea Kasprzak, 2019

BUSINESSES

Katrina Widener Coaching: *Business Community Leader and Entrepreneur Coach*

Show My Your Woo: *A high vibrational community devoted to teaching and sharing all things "woo"*

Lake Anama by Sydney: *Practical self-care and soul-deep healing techniques for reducing stress, improving energy, and manifesting transformation.*

APPENDIX II

GOING ON YOUR OWN OR GETTING HELP

Freelancer Hub

- Fivvr
- Upwork
- Guru
- Passive / Active

Print On Demand

- Printful
- Society6
- RedBubble
- Printly
- Fine Art of America
- Pictorem
- FinerWorks
- Prodigi
- IngramSpark

Marketplace

- Etsy
- Creative Market

MARKETING

Website Domains

- SquareSpace
- Bluehost
- Google Domains
- Domain.com
- Host Gator
- DreamHost
- Shopify

LEGAL

Shopify https://www.shopify.com/tools/policy-generator/terms-and-conditions

Free Privacy Policy https://www.freeprivacypolicy.com/

BIO

Anung is the owner and mastermind behind Courageous Creativity. Which started as a side hustle and turned into a full business by combining a bunch of hustles together. Loves helping others work on their mindset and what's possible with money to fellow misfits and black sheep.

She is also the host of The Introvert's Bubble and I Don't Wanna Fit In podcasts, with more to come. Second half of Podcast du Nord, podcasting conference and learning. Serial starter and dreamer.

She lives in Minnesota with her dog and coworker Enzo. Who has won Employee of the Month for years somehow. Constantly reading, writing, and creating, plus talking to other creatives.

www.ingramcontent.com/pod-product-compliance
Lightning Source LLC
Chambersburg PA
CBHW070044120526
44589CB00035B/2313